ITALY
ONE
HUNDRED
CITIES

PHOTOGRAPHS BY
PEPI MERISIO

TEXT BY
EUGENIO TURRI

ITALY
ONE
HUNDRED
CITIES

TAURIS
PARKE
BOOKS

Photography Credits
The photographs in this volume are all
taken specially, except the following:
Archivio Aerofotografico of the IGMI: 10 (conc.
SMAN no.14 of 12/18/1988), 11 (conc. SMAN no.33 of
9/27/1985), 12 (conc. SMAN no.33 of 8/30/1988), 13
(conc. SMAN no.51 of 12/18/1985), 14 (conc. SMAN
no.153 of 3/8/1971), 15 (conc. SMAN no.49 of
1/16/1970), 19 (conc. SMAN no.52 of 1/18/1984);
Archivio Fabbri: 8, 9;
Compagnia Generale Riprese aeree di Ferretti,
Parma: 17.

First published in the United Kingdom in 1991 by
Tauris Parke Books
110 Gloucester Avenue, London NW1 8JA
in association with KEA Publishing Services Ltd., London

Text copyright © 1990 Amilcare Pizzi SpA.
Photography copyright © 1991 Pepi Merisio

Original Italian language edition *Cento Città*
published by Silvana Editoriale SpA, Milan

The Cataloguing in Publication Data for this book is available
from the British Library, London.
ISBN 1-85043-344-5

⊕ AMILCARE PIZZI EDITORE
Design and Production
by the Editorial Department, Amilcare Pizzi
Director: Massimo Pizzi
Graphics and Layout: Paolo Regini
Editing: A&P Editing
Translation: Andrew Ellis

Printed and bound by Amilcare Pizzi SpA Arti
Grafiche, Cinisello Balsamo, Milan, Italy

Contents

THE CITIES OF ITALY. Foreword

In the chaos of buildings and roads that invades Italy today, where are the historical cities of what was once known as the "bel paese," the beautiful country? Where are the towers, the cathedrals, the palaces of the inner cities which, in centuries past, drew foreign visitors on an artistic pilgrimage that provided an unparalleled concentration of European culture? Nowadays even the towers and belfries of the town centers are hard to make out in the argosy of cranes and concrete cluttering the skylines of the Italian cityscape. The ancient profiles for which each town was known are either hidden from view or utterly humbled beneath the tidal wave of concrete and metal that has wrought havoc throughout Italy in the last forty years.

And yet if, after running the gauntlet of the traffic-choked outer streets, you make it past the shapeless initial wall of buildings, you may still reach the historical core of the old town, guided as if by some irresistible inner voice. You will be rewarded for your pains, as you eventually find yourself among houses and streets that exude history from every cranny, buildings which have set the standards of architectural aesthetics throughout Europe. Once here you will find medieval alleys and porticoes where for centuries the bustle of people has never ceased, street corners where gusts of wind stir the dust in shafts of brilliant sunlight. Finally, you step into the sheer magic of the historical central piazza — be it Piazza Duomo, Piazza Municipio, or Piazza della Signoria — the fulcrum of all the ups and downs of the town's history, consecrated by time's flow. Here stand the glorious churches, the noble palaces and leaning towers of bygone centuries. The piazza is always worth the trouble of finding it.

The very core of the urban community, each piazza is an oasis in an Italy that in the last few decades seems to have done its utmost to smother its heritage. Many of these inner sanctuaries are unscathed (often merely because they were so well cloistered that meddling was almost impossible), and still offer moments of silence and vistas that would otherwise be utterly lost.

Here the observant eye can trace the Italian city's birth and growth, and how it fostered a sense of urban civilization that has provided a model for the whole of Europe through the centuries.

Safely ensconced within a ring of nineteenth-century expansion, outside of which the devastating development policies of recent years have taken their toll, the inner city recounts the entire history of Italy. Here one can follow a story that began with the Romans and came into full flower in the eleventh century, the era of the communes, when every town on the peninsula boasted its own territory and distinct identity. Town life became suddenly important; the spirit of this new and revolutionary *forma urbis* lives on in many town and city centers, especially in smaller towns detached from the main built-up areas, which were scarcely affected by later developments.

The Towered Cities

If you venture along the route of the ancient Roman causeway Via Cassia, which leads from Certaldo in Tuscany to Siena (and thence to Rome), at a certain point you will catch sight of the towers of the famous hilltop town of San Gimignano, one of the most evocative of all those towns whose original communes have managed to survive virtually intact. This first glimpse is unforgettable, one of the finest impressions of Italy, its landscapes, and its geographical and historical uniqueness. With its jutting towers and exquisite formal harmony in stark contrast to the chaos of the modern town, San Gimignano is like a dream city, pieced together from archetypes. Here we begin our tour of Italy's cities, accompanied by the fine photographs of Pepi Merisio. While San Gimignano is one of the peninsula's most outstanding examples of preservation, nearby Certaldo and many other so-called centers of "minor" importance offer unlimited variety to any historical or tourist journey through Italy.

In the Middle Ages, the towers for which San Gimignano is so well-known were common to many Italian towns. Some boasted them in great number — the city of Bologna is supposed to have had over eighty, and Siena, Perugia, and Arezzo each had several dozen. It is not hard to imagine the townscape during the early phases of urbanization, as it is pictured with photographic clarity in the background of paintings by fourteenth- and fifteenth-century masters such as Fra Angelico, Piero della Francesca, Ambrogio Lorenzetti, and Vittorio Carpaccio. Here the town is shown as a complete, enclosed entity — a work of art carefully grafted onto the landscape — in which towers vie with the belfries and pinnacles of the cathedrals for our notice.

While the cathedral was invariably the most prominent building in any town — as a symbol of religious power it stood shoulder-to-shoulder with its civic counterpart, the town hall, which represented the power of the people — a town's real character came from the number and height of its towers. Although towers were relatively new as urban architecture, their economic, social, and cultural role in the community was still more significantly novel, indicating the presence and prestige of the dominating families. This new class of citizen, by controlling its economy, had a firm hold on the destiny of the entire township. The higher the towers were, the more wealthy and powerful were their occupants. While absolute authority remained in the hands of the religious and imperial powers, the *cives* — bourgeois town-dwellers — asserted themselves, flaunting their emancipation to the castle-dwelling feudal lords, who had ruled over both countryside and town while the town lacked economic leverage. Through this "insurrection" of the township, or of its bourgeois class, civic power finally rose to match feudal dominance and the dynamic economy of the tradesmen and artisans stood up to that of the feudal lords.

As with other Italian towns which have managed to preserve their ancient centers, San Gimignano is symbolic of the sweeping revolution of urban culture in Italy and even in modern Europe. Here the stranglehold of the lords was loosened by the multiple and democratic verve of the rising bourgeoisie. To some extent, the new commune foreshadowed the modern, capitalist city with its culmination in the typical American city center, clustered with skyscrapers just as the medieval Italian communes were clustered with towers: Manhattan echoes San Gimignano.

The Italian commune is cogently pictured in Ambrogio Lorenzetti's striking fresco *The Effects of Correct Government* in Siena's town hall. The work is divided into two parts. On the left, the towers and palaces of the walled city rear up, crisscrossed by streets teeming with tradesfolk, shopkeepers, craftsmen, and masons building ever new towers and palaces: the epitome of the lively burg, an industrious manufacturing center governed not by some oppressive power but by free men who have taken the affairs of the town into their own hands. On the right, the countryside unfolds in a succession of rolling hills with scattered farmsteads surrounded by fields of corn and vineyards, cultivated with the same methods used today in certain corners of the Tuscan countryside. Farmers stoop to gather the grain, groups of huntsmen follow their

hounds. In the background we can make out the castle outside the borough, its sovereignty by this time overshadowed by the authority of the commune. Above all, this remarkable fresco pictures clearly how the town related to its *contado* or surrounding castles and hamlets, the whole bound by an active and constant interchange; how, with its ability to pilot the economy, to absorb and harness the productivity of the rural areas, the town could fashion and organize that countryside. The traffic of mules through the city gates, symbolic of this interchange, reiterates the newfound assertion of the urban economy over that of the castle.

The city's definitive imposition across the entire peninsula took place from the eleventh to the fourteenth century, a period in which Italy was defining its sociopolitical geography as the "land of cities." This expression did not simply refer to the concentration of towns or the beauty of their monuments, but to the cogent sense of urban culture that could be felt everywhere, to the role the town played in the organization of space and in the development of the evolved civilization which graced the peninsula for several centuries. Although the communal townships would later pass into the clutches of the noblemen and princes who sprang from the more influential tower-dwelling families as they jostled for control of the urban

economy, these centuries witnessed the emergence of Italy as we know it.

An Urban Dendrochronology

The background of the Italian town that we can trace in the many small towns and ancient city centers is only one aspect of the dense subsoil of history from which the city itself draws its nourishment, laid in successive strata over the original nucleus of the main piazza, a nucleus whose form often retraces the original Roman plan.

The Romans were prodigious town-builders; their highly functional and precise planning can be recognized even today in the older sections of certain Italian towns and cities. The main clue is the road grid, which in Roman times was based on two main thoroughfares — the *cardum* and *decumanum* — giving a simplified geometrical layout to the town. The point where these two thoroughfares met was considered sacred land, reserved for temples and the *forum*, the quintessential public building representing the entire urban territory, including outlying lands in the town's jurisdiction. The medieval central piazza crystallized around this Roman grid, often borrowing stone from disused temples for the construction of new houses and palaces. In Lucca, for instance, the Roman town plan is not

only unmistakable in the layout of the streets but also, astonishingly, in the splendid shape of Piazza del Mercato, which grew out of the ellipse of an ancient amphitheater. Geometrical structures echoing the layout of Roman towns can be found in Florence, Bologna, Modena, Verona, and Turin. Elsewhere, the relics of Roman buildings testify eloquently to a city's antiquity, as in Rome, Benevento, and Aosta, blending in with the evolving urban landscape.

After the era of the communes, Italy's towns by no means betrayed their past. They may have renewed and reconstructed the buildings, but the layout of streets and squares has largely endured. At the same time, the towns inevitably fleshed out. In Florence, for instance, a series of new rings grew around the original square of the Roman *urbs* near the Arno river. The first ring marks the expansion of the early commune, cradled within its twelfth-century walls, outside of which there grew a second ring; this in turn was enclosed within walls built during the thirteenth and fourteenth centuries. Further growth came about in more recent times, particularly during the expansion of the 1800s — when Florence briefly became the capital of the newly united Italy — and, of course, in this century. In general, Italy's major cities have continued to swell in all directions; less prominent towns have been left almost intact, as if certain trees in a forest had enjoyed

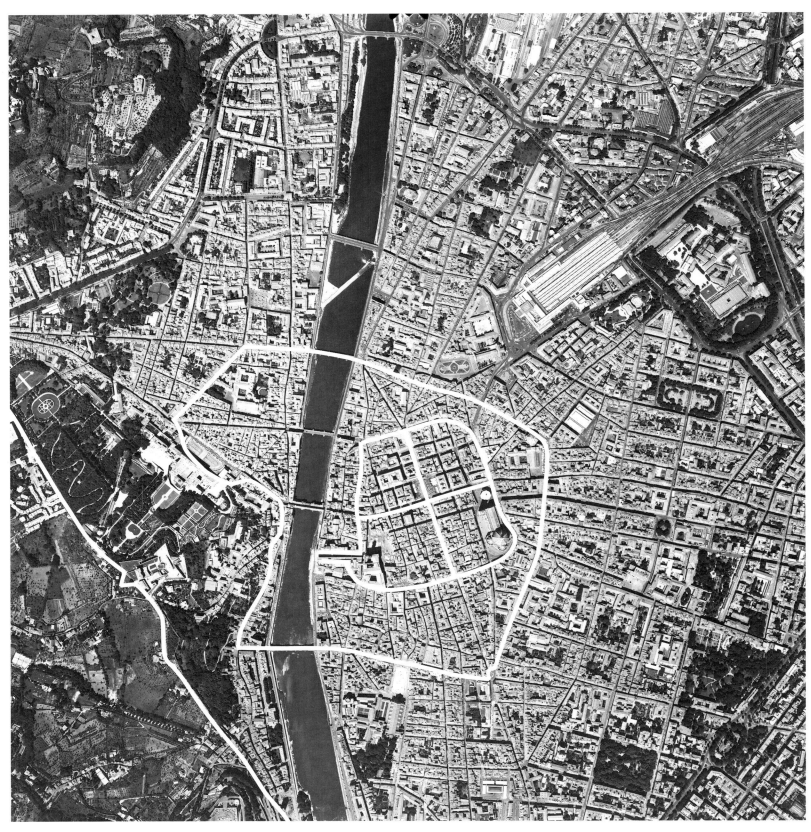

unimpeded growth, overshadowing the rest so they remain slender and less imposing. Indeed, the concentric belts of expansion in Italian cities are not unlike the growth rings of a tree. And as in plant dendrochronology each ring provides a precise guide to periods of drought or abundant rainfall, each urban ring offers clues to the prosperity or economic stringency of its era of growth. The study of urban expansion is a kind of urban dendrochronology through which we can trace the history of the changing urban landscape as the city passes through cycles of hardship and fortune. Some Italian towns seem to have suffered recessions in certain periods, where others continued to grow. This can be detected in the quality and styles of the buildings themselves, whether churches, palazzi, or ordinary houses. The inexorable path of growth is most strikingly revealed in Milan, with its combination of Roman relics and vestiges of medieval and Renaissance prosperousness, followed by development undertaken in the last three centuries. This extraordinary layering of history betrays the irrepressible enterprising spirit of Lombardy's capital, situated in the heart of the most vital area of the Po Valley plains. Further east, the city of Verona also offers a

■ Florence's layout clearly shows the three successive perimeter walls around which the city developed in stages. The first walls date from Roman times, and those after from the Middle Ages (eleventh to fourteenth centuries).

■ As the picture shows, the structure of the lagoon town of Chioggia is based on a rectangular grid flanked by the Canale della Vena. Although the basic plan is more regular and geometrical, the town is a smaller version of Venice.

wealth of history, with exemplary fragments of Roman and medieval architecture (dating from the communes and the era of the Scala family) and, not least, buildings in the regional Renaissance style. Other periods, however, such as the eighteenth and nineteenth centuries are poorly documented here. Venice, on the other hand, is lacking in Roman monuments: the city really came into being in the late Middle Ages, its original nucleus formed in the eleventh century on an island corresponding to today's Piazza San Marco. This nucleus gradually fleshed out with row upon row of palaces testifying to the style of each

era — Gothic, Renaissance, seventeenth- and eighteenth-century — along the Canal Grande and the other waterways of this magical city. The nearby town of Chioggia, though structured around a main street and not a canal, offers another example of the classic lagoon city, a latter-day Venice. Rome presents an entirely different story. With different centers of urban growth strewn across its seven hills, over the centuries Rome has expanded in a far from orderly fashion; still, it tends to cluster around the original nuclei of the ancient city.

Although they too have enjoyed steady growth over the

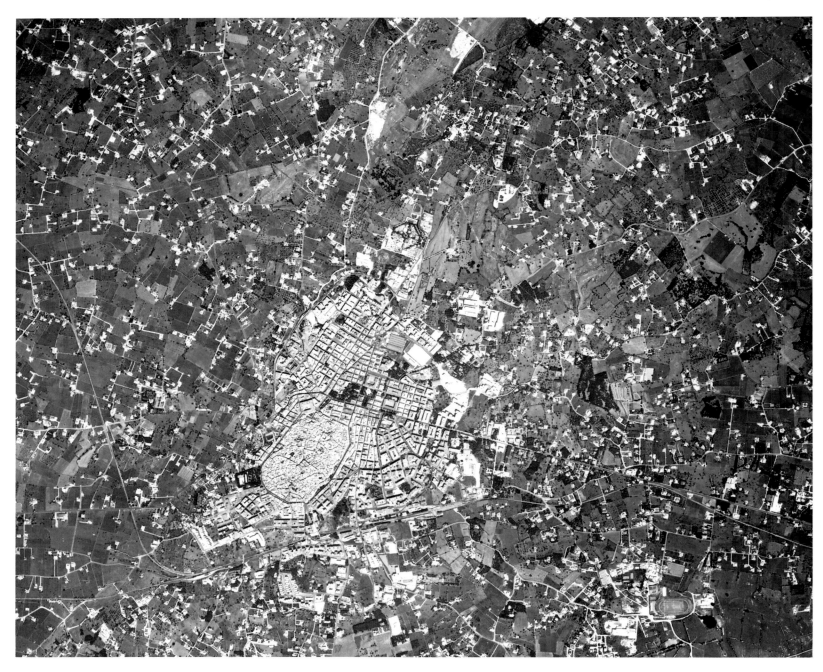

centuries, the cities of the south differ slightly from those of central and northern Italy. Many southern towns crystallized around a medieval nucleus. This is invariably defined by the ancient walls enclosing it, though in many cases these have been replaced by wide roads or streets delimiting the old and the new. This is particularly noticeable in towns throughout Apulia, and in Sicily also, as at Palermo and Catania. The "urban dendrochronology" of Naples, the metropolis of the south, provides far fewer clues, though it is not entirely illegible. Much of the original structure has been overrun by modern development, which has often erased the original urban texture while leaving a sharp distinction between the original medieval nucleus near the harbor and later developments crowding behind what has been called the "finest bay in the world."

Urban Form

After the age of the communes, the next important chapter of development was the Renaissance, from the fifteenth to the eighteenth century, during which the "hundred cities" of Italy reached the peak of their glory.

(Little further progress was made during the nineteenth century, except in Milan and other towns across the Po Valley.) During the Renaissance, the old communal organization of the town was logically carried through on an urban level; economically the town fell under the dominion of a lord or dynast, each one imposing his own laws on the town and its environs. The new lords exercised their control over the townsfolk with prudence and were judicious in their levies, ever careful not to suffocate the forces on which the economy depended. Thus emerged the first of the princely states, the forerunners of today's modern nation state. As seat of the prince's power, the town became the emblem of the magnificence and wealth of the state it embodied. Embellishments and fortifications were made, emphasizing its role as the focus of power. The towers belonging to the earlier bourgeoisie were torn down, and in their place were erected the princely palaces, symbols of the city just as much as the cathedral.

A prime example of the resurgence of the Renaissance town is Urbino, home of the princes of Montefeltro. In the fifteenth century, the medieval town saw the construction of the superb ducal palace, the prestigious residence of the

town's seigneury. The palace was like another town super-imposed on the existing one, a place where culture ruled supreme, where master painters and literary figures were frequent guests. The Renaissance was an era of great sensitivity toward the value of urban culture, which absorbed most of the economic resources of the state. Renaissance palaces and residences of the town lords can be found in almost all the states, republics, dukedoms and princedoms of which Italy was constituted between the fifteenth and eighteenth centuries — Milan, Ferrara, Mantua, Parma, Verona, Venice, Genoa, and Turin. The characteristic growth of northern and central Italy, however, does not apply to the south. Southern towns are distinctive not only for the sheer luminosity of the skies under which they grew, but also for the architecture of the houses themselves, with their blinding whitewashed walls. Even the relationships between the town's buildings — the groupings and spaces which reflect the distribution of power — are different. The southern town did not grow like San Gimignano, with a skyward explosion of towers. South of Lazio, towers were few and far between. Instead, the towns are tightly clustered on hilltops or scattered across the mountainside. Although in the Middle Ages there was no dearth of lively townships in the south — such as the coastal town of Amalfi — they lacked the forward momentum of the bourgeoisie which had brought prosperity to the central and northern towns. Instead, the old serf system lingered, as attested by the massive manorial castles dominating many of the hilltop towns, and the power of the aristocrats suffocated much of the potential from the lower classes. But other factors set the southern town apart: political (interference from outside, such as the Spanish domination), economic (a more complete exploitation of the land by the seigneurs), and health-related (malaria was rife in the coastal plains and even inland). The very remoteness of southern towns, huddled within their walls or isolated on the mountainsides, is an eloquent testimony to their closure to the outside world and their defensiveness toward change. This enduring insularity has endowed southern towns with an appearance of homogeneity, except for the southern capitals of Naples and Palermo, which, until the end of the eighteenth century, were more economically and culturally animated than many large towns of the north.

From the fifteenth to the eighteenth century, the growth of Italy's towns and cities was matched by a remarkable surge of interest in town planning itself, during which new and unequaled models for city design were put forward. Architects and planners dreamed up their ideal cities, drafted imaginative plans, and sometimes even managed to realize them. New defense systems were devised, new types of piazzas, new street layouts, and of course new buildings and cathedrals. Their inventors, the fathers of Italy's glorious artistic production, included Leonardo da Vinci, Leon Battista Alberti, Michelangelo, and Bramante. Attention turned to utopian visions — architects believed they could redesign the world, make it safer and more beautiful. Among the most prominent realizations are defense systems such as the walls enclosing the medieval burg of Lucca, one of the finest examples in Italy. Other cities redesigned from the point of view of military defense include the remarkable star-shaped town of Palmanova in the Friuli plains, its double walls, dry moat, and bastions encompassing a perfectly regular, geometrical town plan. In stark contrast, the town of Sabbioneta, near Mantua, was built by the Gonzaga family with an eye to grace rather than tactical advantage. But one of the most magnificent feats of all, which signaled a completely novel perception of town construction, was the enlargement scheme for the town of Ferrara. Seat of the dukedom of the Este family, Ferrara's existing nucleus was enhanced by means of an ingeniously devised addition, known as the "Addizione Erculea," planned by the architect Biagio Rossetti in the sixteenth century. A network of regular, open streets grafted onto the original street plan, the Addizione Erculea provides a seamless transition from the old town to the new, from one world to another, and opened the town up spatially to the new age, to accommodate all future enlarge-

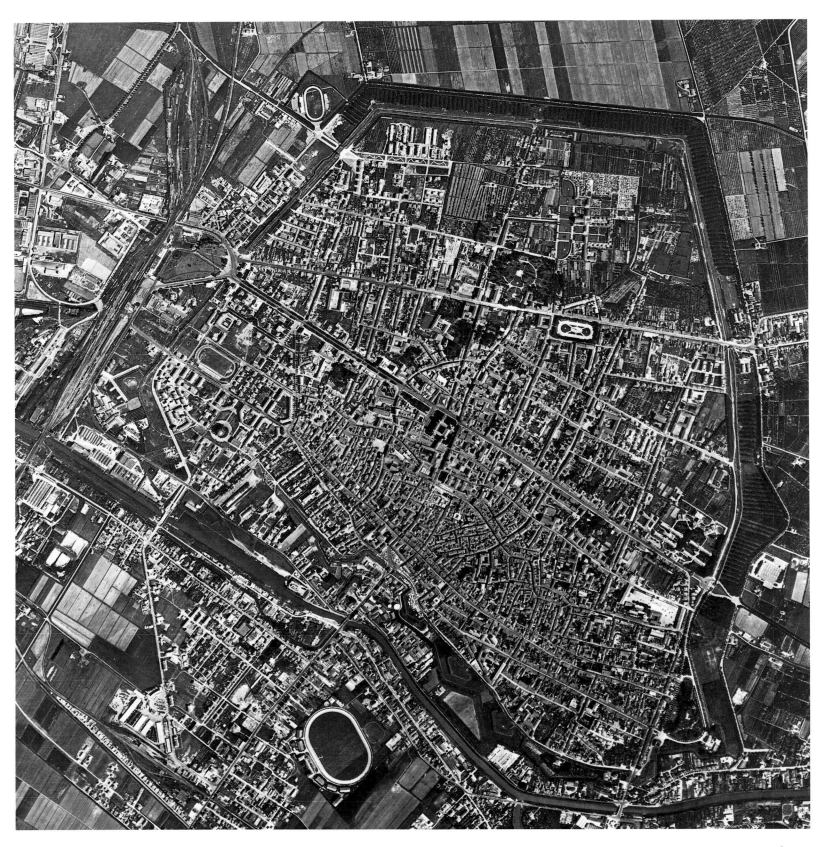

ment of the town. Rossetti's scheme — repeated elsewhere, and not only in Italy — represented a truly revolutionary concept, and marked the end of the Middle Ages and its cloistered, inward-looking town plan.

Urban Scenographies

In addition to the marvels of planning, the period through the Renaissance to the eighteenth century witnessed the triumph of architecture. Churches of inimitable beauty were erected, embodying as no other kind of edifice can the building skills and aspirations of the populace. Italian towns are blessed with dozens of churches, both small and large, many of exquisite charm, but it is in the *duomo* or cathedral that the main ambitions of the community are most clearly read. Usually the cathedral sets the tone of the entire cityscape, asserting the architectural style and even the type of materials (such as local stone and marble) to be used around it.

The inventory of churches which ennoble the Italian townscape is endless. Romanesque churches, perhaps the most typically Italian, derive their form from the canons of

14

■ The layout of Ferrara: the medieval town is enhanced by the famous Addizione Erculea created during the Renaissance by Biagio Rossetti in the first example of modern town planning in Europa. The two parts of the town meet along a central corridor formed by Via Cavour and Corso della Giovecca.

■ The Sicilian town of Grammichele, with its characteristic hexagonal, concentric plan. It was founded in 1693 by the Prince of Butera and Roccella to harbor the inhabitants of his feudal property Occhiolà, destroyed by an earthquake. The prince drafted the town plan himself, basing it on the advanced principles of Enlightenment thinking.

Roman architecture. The solutions available within the Romanesque style, however, are many and often vary from region to region — in some cases even town to town. The originality of certain examples is occasionally due to rivalry between parishes, a throwback from the days of the communes. The Romanesque churches of Apulia, Umbria, and Tuscany are often tinged with Gothic touches and are quite different from those of the Po river plains (as in Modena, Parma, and Verona), not to mention the church of Saint Ambrose in Milan, considered the greatest achievement of this particular architectural form. The Romanesque is fol-lowed by the Renaissance style; the Renaissance churches of Florence break entirely new ground with their exquisitely pure lines, and have their ultimate expression in the cupola of Florence's cathedral, a masterpiece of engineering by Brunelleschi that, perhaps more than any other building, epitomizes the spirit of Renaissance architecture. Representing a new form of structure conceived of lightness and intelligence and striving to establish a new relation between mankind and nature, this towering feat of engineering both embraces and gives tone to the city, providing a synthesis of the new harmonic vision that

15

bound town planning to architecture, and architecture to the landscape.

Other settings of extraordinary scenic power include Pisa's Piazza dei Miracoli, where the duomo, baptistery, and leaning tower offer a trinity in pure Carrara marble celebrating the wisdom and refinement of a city which was once a leading seaport. Like neighboring Umbria, the region of Tuscany abounds with towns whose monuments merge harmoniously in exceptional settings, where the main house of worship is set in the piazza as if it were the home of everyone, a symbol of perfection and a synthesis of all that has preceded it. Such remarkable cathedral squares can be found in Pistoia, Lucca, Prato, and Arezzo, to name but a few. The same goes for the central piazzas of towns in the Po Valley and Veneto region, and many towns throughout central Italy.

Rome, however, is different. Rome's churches are its main treasure. Some rise out of the ruins of Roman temples; others present Renaissance or baroque features deftly woven with the ancient ruins around them. With its cupola by Michelangelo, the Renaissance masterpiece of Saint Peter's is one of a kind. Its novel design anticipates the movements of later centuries, which find their utmost expression in the glorious baroque cathedrals of the southern towns, where the magnetic influence of the Mediterranean is expressed in a more sanguine design, in the decorative excesses of an art replete with Spanish influence.

After the house of worship, the next most important architectural feature of the urban scenery is the palazzo, which includes not only the princely residences but also the houses of nobility and the moneyed middle class. Perhaps there is nothing anywhere to compare with the sheer splendor of the palazzi lining Venice's imposing Canal Grande, which was designed to celebrate the power and prestige of the Venetian nobility. To this day, these buildings continue to compete in beauty and monumental grandeur. Monuments to the prosperity of their owners, the palazzi of the Canal Grande are tokens of a pleasure in building which was virtually unrivaled from the fifteenth to the eighteenth century; yet all the towns of the Veneto region boast a splendid collection of noble buildings. Vicenza, for one, is a virtuoso array of grandiose palaces, many judiciously styled according to the canons of the area's principal architect, Andrea Palladio.

In Milan the buildings reflect the inherent industriousness of a serious-minded middle class, which rejected ostentation in favor of a more entrepreneurial luster in its building style. By contrast, in southern Italy, princes and barons left over from the *ancien régime* squandered riches accumulated from vast feudal lands, which soon became landed estates dotted with townhouses where distinction and nobility was expressed by an explosion of baroque whimsy. The style prevailed not only in Naples, Palermo, and Catania, but also in smaller towns where the nobleman

could parade his culture and tastes — often with European (as opposed to Mediterranean) overtones — by creating grandiose palazzi, like those in Noto and Modica.

But towns are not composed of individual buildings, churches, or fine palazzi. Towns are a complex patchwork of mass and void, avenues and tight alleys, piazzas and passageways. Every town has its own scenery, its own way of accenting its churches, towers, and palaces, depending as much on its basic structure as on its location. Southern towns are generally more simply laid out. This is mainly due to the regime of ownership that, since the eighteenth century, was tied to a system of farming that brought hundreds upon hundreds of families together as serfs under a seigneur or landlord. At times such aggregations dubbed "farmer townships," were composed of small identical buildings symmetrically displaced around the duomo or the landlord's residence. A good example is Grammichele, an extensive, concentric eighteenth-century settlement laid out according to the ideas of its Enlightenment landlord, who came from Ragusa, Sicily. A very different approach is seen in central and northern Italy, where the differentiation of towns stems from the steady growth and shifts in style, with new churches and palazzi replacing old ones, together with the reworking of the streets, road system and piazzas.

The concentric layout is common to most of Italy's historical towns, which are invariably structured around a central square, site of the duomo or city hall. These historical squares remain the most striking feature of the Italian town plan, and offer their citizens a kind of *salotto* or open-air foyer set against a backcloth of outstanding palazzi and monumental architecture embodying the town's history and culture.

The stones bear the imprint of the past; the setting, together with the silhouette of the hills that surround it, becomes the image of the town's spirit. The town nestles like a living organism in its landscape: Florence, wrote Guy de Maupassant, was where he would "most have liked to live, a city that spells ineffable *charme* to my eyes and my heart, drawing me to it like a woman, reclining, the epitome of carnal appeal. When I think of this city, so full of marvels, where one retires at the end of a day drained from observation, like a huntsman tired from the chase, she suddenly seems to glow, and impressions of her dance about in my mind's eye, and seems like a large, long curtain against which, like some *grande dame*, the city reclines, shamelessly, naked and blonde, alert and tranquil."

Man and the City

With their palazzi, districts, and streets arranged organically around the central piazza, Italy's towns are busy and lively. Side-by-side, craftsmen, tradesmen, administrators, members of the cloth, nobles and ordinary civilians, rich or poor, go about their business. Although it forms a

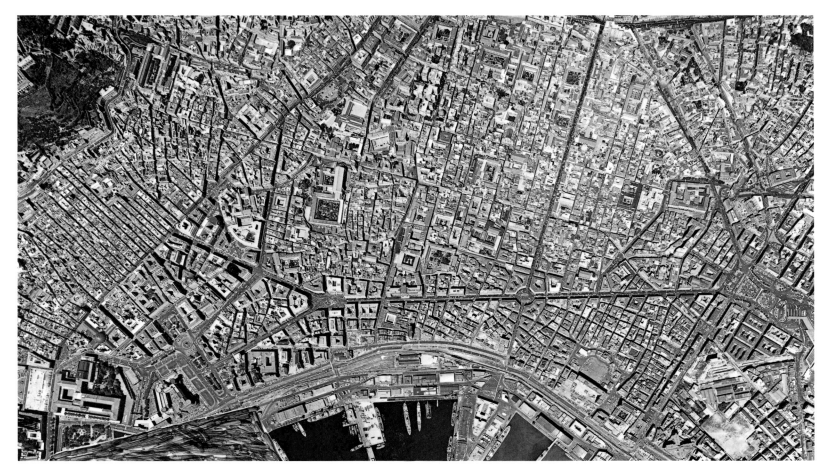

cohesive whole, the Italian town has segregated people socially, from the outset. But ever since the days of the communes, it has continued to make room for people, coaxing out their qualities. Here, community feeling finds an apposite seedbed in the closeness of the houses, the central arrangement of the town square and high street — these are public places, places to meet under the shadow of the noble palazzi.

Craftsmen have always been of prime social importance in Italy and are largely responsible for its urban culture. The urban setting offered artisans the ideal context for going about their work. They gathered in the towns, forming guilds, associations and corporations occupying one or more streets. Even today many streets throughout the country carry the name of the old guilds, a reminder of the crucial role crafts played in town life, where the economy was largely based on the transformation of produce brought in from the countryside and on the sale of manufactured goods in shops or fairs and markets. The towns also staged weekly or daily markets, not unlike those that continue to enliven today's town centers. The vendors seem to have inherited some antique art of salesmanship, an innate ability to communicate and haggle with their buyers. Such markets frequently seem to be something of the past, as if outside the flux of time.

This sense of the past is especially strong in and around places of worship, now often somewhat detached since they lost their central role in urban life. In the hushed church interiors, old women, kneeling in prayer, uphold ancient habits. Time is suspended in an incomparable silence, interrupted only by the weekly program of religious ceremonies and Masses, the notes of the organ, sermons, and halting confessions. But the social spirit of the church and its buoyant humanity come into their own in the square outside, under the shadow of the towers and belfries where for

centuries the townsfolk have gone through the same rites and gestures: greeting acquaintances, pausing for reflection or stopping to chat, whiling away an idle hour and sometimes shirking work. The pavement of these squares is often worn smooth. Here and there, the shadow of grime on the buildings is a reminder of the passage of the townsfolk, their idling, and their unshakable attachment to the town square.

For centuries, the people of Verona have paraded up and down the busy promenade at Piazza Bra. The locals call the promenade the *liston*, and its locally quarried stone pitted with fossils is worn smooth by the endless train of young people who consider it a kind of mating ground, and have as long as anyone can remember. Goethe and other travelers have described Verona's well-to-do youths in their hansom carriages, pausing to chat with the young women and secure the promise of a rendezvous. What took place two centuries ago is repeated today, with the main difference being that the hansom has been replaced by the latest in four-wheel drive vehicles.

Farther south, in the busy town of Ascoli Piceno, the spacious Piazza del Popolo has long since been closed to traffic. Mornings and weekends the square is animated by local gentlemen, gathered in random groups, talking and swapping news. The gentle buzzing sound that hovers over the square today has perhaps changed little over the centuries. Every piazza, every street, has its own peculiar sound, its own characteristic chatter and rhythmic coming and going. The streets of Naples resound with the cries of people greeting each other and debating: a hubbub of human exchange testifying to the vitality and human drama of which the city is constituted. Vivacity is a common characteristic of southern towns. Here the people live very much out in the open, a fact invariably noted by travelers in earlier days, aghast at finding such extrovert and noisy

17

goings-on, which they attributed to the climate. There is certainly a degree of truth in all this. The habits of the south are centuries-old, like the afternoon parade round the central piazza or along the high street, nicknamed *struscio* because of the typical crawling, dragging gait and idle exchange of glances, which sometimes trigger a sudden flushing of cheeks. Here the town's youth struts and swaggers, or, as the poet Giacomo Leopardi put it, *"per le vie si spande; e mira ed è mirata, e in cor s'allegra"* (they saunter down the streets, admiring and being admired, their hearts athrill). Away from these squares and streets at the heart of town life, the outskirts offer deserted, out-of-the-way lanes and hidden piazzas where life seems to be suspended in an atmosphere of rarefied forgetfulness and silence. In these secluded corners people are apparently unchanged, untouched by the passage of time. Venice's quiet backwaters have something decidedly arcane about them, a dreamlike atmosphere no other Italian town can match. Here, the town can seem like an oasis from the deafening chaos of the traffic-choked streets and modern worries.

Today there is a growing effort to stem the invasion of cars and concrete for which Italian towns have, regrettably, become famous, an invasion which has cost them their identity, their distinctive features, canceling a past of singular vitality. The threat of losing this identity has spurred some towns to revive public festivals and rites that once reverberated through every street. Often enough the main objective is to draw tourists, but in many cases the locals still participate in these festivals as they did hundreds of years ago, despite media intrusions and tourism. Although the famous Palio in Siena's central piazza is covered by the television and newspapers, the race remains a deeply-felt experience for the local population; with its echoes of the early communes and the rivalry between boroughs, the Palio embodies a sense of enduring tradition. Once, religious processions were a major feature of town life. Today, most of these pageants have been discontinued, except in the south, where religious feeling and worship have remained part of the daily business of living. All these public displays and rituals — the pageants, processions, and festivals — are not enough to restore the town to its former glory: they are brief and illusory intervals in an urban environment besieged by unsolved problems of traffic, pollution, mismanagement, and decaying monuments. Every town has become a problem in itself. There have always been problems — social discrimination, pockets of abject poverty, economic instability — but the advent of industrialization and changes in the Italian lifestyle has added its own unique traumas.

The Industrial City and the Suffocation of the Historical Center

Industrialism made its first appearance on the Italian landscape in the last century. Few towns were affected initially; Milan was at the center of the new revolution, and after the Unification became the economic keystone of the nation, asserting its own brand of business-oriented, industrial mystique on the rest of the country. It also opened Italy to other cultures across the Alps, allowing European influence to filter down through Lombardy and into the rest of the country. Nor did the city overlook the lessons of the Hapsburg and other central European cultures. Milan has since spun a web of metropolitan development that includes many surrounding towns like Varese and Bergamo, creating a dynamic urbanized area of five to six million inhabitants, one of the most extensive in Europe.

Another city caught in the industrialization process was Turin, formerly the capital of the little state of Savoy and instigator of the movement for the political unification of Italy. Essentially an Alpine city, Turin is governed by a severe logic confirmed by its geometrical layout and baroque monuments.

The third pole in the "industrial triangle," Genoa — "La Superba" — with its barrage of buildings perched along the rocky seafront, was the most vital in the early phases of industrialization because of its key role as a supply-line to the Po Valley.

The rest of Italy's towns and cities experienced halting growth during the first phase of industrialization, largely tied to the role they had assumed in the bureaucracy as regional or provincial capitals. There are currently ninety-six of these; another four due to join them presently will make a total of one hundred, the number of cities for which Italy used to be famous. This round figure of course excludes many smaller centers that, despite their size, boast a history to rival larger centers that have been more fortunate on an economic or administrative level, reflecting the parceling out of land exercised by the communes. The small and medium-sized towns really began to grow only in this century independently from the extent of industry in their midst. In the south growth has been more closely linked to bureaucracy than to real economy, while in the north and Tuscany industry of all sizes was a major force in urban development. Sometimes enterprise has taken its toll, such as the huge chemical plant of Marghera, a stone's throw from Venice, where the two worlds of art and industry, of historical wisdom and chemical engineering, stand in diabolical contrast. The post-industrial world seems to have come to terms with this clash, despite the problem of pollution, as yet irremediable.

Industry is not alone in defiling the image of the Italian city. The population growth, once checked by Fascist regulations, simply exploded in the second half of this century in the wake of the "economic miracle." The main aftermath was an exodus from the countryside, with a consequent proliferation of sprawl in the outer city during the economic, political, and social revolutions of the 1960s and 1970s. Government control of growth was irresolute and proved incapable of safeguarding the country's urban heri-

tage or creatively grafting the new city onto the old — a dismal betrayal of Biagio Rossetti's brilliant legacy. Burgeoning industrial development subsequently spilled into the periphery, encroaching on land where it did not belong and introducing new standards for building and new ways of perceiving the human artifact, contrary to everything the country's past had taught in terms of manual craftsmanship and human ingenuity. It was all inevitable; inevitable, too, the uncontrolled cordons of new housing projects, frequently created through studied speculation on cheap agricultural land on the city fringes. Lost also was the opportunity of creating a rational and sensible road network that did not destroy the ancient hearts of Italy's towns, when it would be quite sufficient to close them to traffic and create efficient links with the expanding suburban areas.

Today we are beginning to realize that the Italian town is caught in a stranglehold — and many are already quite dead. An answer to traffic congestion is absolutely essential, together with the issues of housing blight and the decay of both our monuments and our society. Much of this destruction was brought about by the recent waves of monstrous, formless developments. Our cities can be saved by restoring dignity to the historical centers, by retrieving the inherent beauty and human dimension of this irreplaceable heritage. Only then will the identity of the country be safe.

The economic growth of Italy, one of the richest and most industrialized countries in the world, has little mean-

ing if, in the process of growing, it fails to rescue its vast legacy, if it forgets the communes with their towered skylines. Speaking on the question of the "time of space" and on how to safeguard "time" in the spaces we have, the eminent town planner K. Lynch pointed the way: we must restore dignity to the country's heritage, now lacerated by the ravages of time and history. We must find a proper location for the past within the constant flux of time. This applies as much to architecture as to our towns and cities, the historical centers, which remain a sacred feature of the country's geography.

Eugenio Turri

THE ALPINE CITIES. The Defense of Identity

*P*eople tend to think of the Alpine valleys as a region populated exclusively by small settlements scattered through the hillsides and valleys. Towns are seldom considered an important feature of the Alps. And yet built-up areas are quite at home in the Alpine valleys and have features all their own, as much on the northern slopes as on the Italian side. There are no large valleys in the Alps without inhabited areas of some sort; though never full-fledged cities as such, each town is an expression of the valley geography, with its spatial limits to growth. This lack of size is well compensated by grace, a civil atmosphere, and originality.

Alpine towns in Italy vary considerably because they always reflect their location — a sweeping valley or hillside — and have few links with other towns on the same side of the mountain. They reflect an awareness of the territories outside the Alps with which they communicate, serving as mediation points for transalpine traffic and maintaining communication links between one side and the other of the mountain chain, or between the mountainside and the plain. Due to their role of go-between, the valleys are exposed to the openings and influences of other civilizations. But all this goes on under the vigilant eye of the highlanders, who never lose a sense of their identity and use it as a yardstick for deciding what to welcome and what to rebuff. In this way the villages and towns in the Alps have managed for centuries to remain focuses of an original lifestyle that, while open to communication from outside, never loses sight of highland values. As an eminent Italian scholar of the Alpine world, Giotto Dainelli, has observed, "If you bring together people with a different level of culture and different everyday rhythms, each one has its qualities and its defects. But whichever has a lower level of culture and a relatively more simple or even primitive lifestyle will tend to absorb the other's defects before its qualities. Instead, people who live among the mountains have — or, at least, used to have — an astonishing resistance to change: they have clung to their defects, but also to their virtues." This applies to inhabitants of Alpine villages and towns alike.

Alpine towns are necessarily different from those of the plain. The tastes and passions of highland culture can be sensed everywhere. The houses themselves follow certain building patterns and public buildings are given the utmost prominence. Behavior everywhere is conspicuously civil, and in every street and square there is a lingering sense of severity. But has this atmosphere actually managed to survive in the hillside towns? Here as elsewhere in Italy the upheavals of this century have destroyed much of the country's former authenticity. Alpine towns have also experienced radical transformations, albeit in smaller measure. The industrial, consumer-oriented influence of the Po Valley has percolated through into some of the surrounding valleys, leaving them with a jumbled patchwork of houses and factories. Some towns, like Cortina d'Ampezzo, have become venues for summer vacationers or important winter ski resorts. But despite encroaching modernization, the original character of each town endures in the historical core, echoing its original function as a bridge between the more remote mountain communities and the main valley roads that usher traffic across the mountain range and beyond. The past lives on in Aosta, with its fine Roman relics, and the same may be said for Bressanone, Bolzano and Trent, with their enchanting town centers and fine churches. Bormio, likewise, cradled in the great Rhetian valley, conserves a vibrant past. Towns like these are best defined as Alpine, and only partially Italian — especially those along the main route through Upper Adige, where the clusters of Tyrolean-style houses brace themselves with true highland tenacity.

1. The Roman city walls of Aosta, against the steep southern slope of the sweeping valley named after the town. The medieval tower of Baillage, built from the spoils of nearby Roman ruins, can be seen behind them. Aosta's Roman birthright testifies to the town's longstanding prominence as a strategic outpost along the main routes across the Alps. Aosta in fact lies on the route to the Great Saint Bernard pass, one of the most important crossings of the entire Alpine chain. Lower down another road leads off to the Small Saint Bernard pass. Even today, the role of the town — the capital of the Valle d'Aosta, one of the richest regions in Italy — is closely tied to its geographical position and emphasized by the road and motorway links and the tunnel through Mont Blanc. But this role is also a burden, and threatens to impair the town's former appeal. Some solace remains in the relics and vestiges of Rome, which recount the town's ancestry and its history as a crossroads for Alpine traffic.

■ 2. Left: A fountain sculpted from granite in Piazza Quadrivio in the center of Sondrio, the small but prosperous capital of the Valtellina province. Despite its growth in this century as a center of administration, business, and commerce, Sondrio has retained many of the features typical of towns in the Valtellina — the highland charm of the churches, houses and venerable old stones, and that unmistakable valley style with its clean, almost Swiss flavor. Historically, Sondrio, like the rest of this section of the valley, was exposed to the Reformist influences of the Grisons, who dominated the valley from the beginning of the sixteenth century to the end of the eighteenth. Apart from these experiences, typical along the frontiers between countries, Sondrio and the Valtellina have an authentic valley culture of their own, a culture which has only just begun to lose its bloom with the irruption of burgeoning industrialization.

■ 3. Frescoes on one of the "two houses of the Duomo" looking out across Piazza Cesare Battisti (otherwise known as Piazza Duomo) in Trent. The frescoes are the handiwork of Matteo Fogolino, a painter from the Friuli region, active in Trent in the early sixteenth century, who contributed to the embellishment of the town's facades. Trent's tone also derives from the many other splendors of Renaissance architecture, its noble bearing largely ascribable to the period in which the town became Italian, under Clesius, prince and bishop of Bressanone. He and his successors in fact harbingered the decline of the Germanic influence in favor of the more advanced culture of the day. The old town center is virtually intact, though hemmed in by extensive development, which has occupied the entire valley floor.

■ 4. Left: A view of Merano against the Giogaia di Tessa, an imposing bastion of Dolomitic crags. The spire alongside the cathedral is a good eighty-three meters high. This town, cradled between the confluence of the Val Passiria and the Valle dell'Adige, has the neatness, style, and noble air peculiar to the Tyrol. Its historical nucleus is a rich inventory of the town's past, which reached its peak between the thirteenth and fourteenth centuries under the counts of Venosta (or Tirolo). Special attractions include the old houses along Via Portici, the castle built during the Austrian occupation, and the cathedral, dating from the fourteenth and fifteenth centuries.

■ 5. Old porticoed houses in the center of Bressanone, a picturesque little town in Upper Adige. Cloistered by its perimeter wall, the old nucleus conserves its alleys, tight corners, passageways, piazzas, and open spaces, and not least its sturdy Tyrolean houses in Gothic style. The cathedral, where Gothic and Romanesque are interwoven, also deserves attention. The complex grouping of buildings, which include the palace of the bishop princes, is a reminder that for several centuries Bressanone was the capital of a princedom controlled by the bishops who ruled the Tyrol. The town was set up as the base of the bishopric before the eleventh century, and the princedom, with its centuries-long patronage of the arts, was only abolished in the last century when the land passed to secular dominion and became part of Austria.

■ 6. Left: The charm of the Gothic and baroque architecture of Bolzano, the main town of the Upper Adige, against the cordon of mountains looming above this important branch in the valley where the Talvera river flows into the Isarco and thence into the Adige itself. Bolzano owes its fortune to this geographical setting. Ever since the Middle Ages the town played a prominent role in trade, and was repeatedly contended by the bishops of Trent and the Tyrolean counts. When the latter forced their dominion on the town in the thirteenth century, the area began to absorb the Germanic influence that has radically changed the life and culture of the town. Perhaps due to this eventful background, Bolzano became the heart of the Tyrol's struggle for autonomy. Insurrection was rife in the eighteenth century and made a comeback in the last century, when Andreas Hofer led an uprising against the Bavarian dominion. Today, despite the Italianization drive initiated during the Fascist era, Bolzano clings to its original culture, to its autonomy.

■ 7. The elegant promenade in Cortina d'Ampezzo, the most celebrated winter resort and ski center in the Dolomites. Despite its relatively reduced dimensions, Cortina is a full-fledged town with amenities of all kinds to cater for the busy winter and summer seasons. The prestigious hotels are complemented by villas owned by wealthy industrial magnates, financial scions and cultural figures from Italy and abroad. Consequently, it has become a kind of appendix to Milan and Rome. But the fabulous backdrop of mountains encircling it, its spectacular ski slopes, and its network of trekking routes make it one of the most splendid venues of the Alps.

■ 8. Overleaf: Glorenza, snugly sited beneath the alluvial cone of the upper Val Venosta. This small and enchanting town has preserved its medieval spirit, with its porticoed houses, gateways, and narrow streets. It was founded in the twelfth century by the counts of Tyrol whose dominion extended this far. They made Glorenza a fortified outpost for overseeing the trade routes and an important emporium for products, especially salt. From the fourteenth century until the last century the town belonged to the Trapp counts, who are largely responsible for the conservation of the town's medieval heritage.

THE CITIES OF PIEDMONT. Stronghold of the Savoy Spirit

*A*lthough they all bear the unmistakable seal of the royal house of Savoy, the towns of Piedmont have their roots in more remote times. Turin itself crystallized around the original quadrilateral plan of a Roman castrum, but the rest of Piedmont's towns are by and large medieval and consequently, from Asti to Ivrea, august towers bear witness to the former glory of the communes. Later, the Savoy legacy clothed each town with a new identity, an identity that has endured in time like a hallmark. This does not simply apply to the main buildings, the rigorous town planning, and the baroque monuments, nor even to the regal, somber mien of the palaces. The influence lies deeper, in the self-awareness they acquired as part of the Savoy political dynasty, as Piedmontese towns strategically sited on the routes through the Alpine valleys, each one encapsulating the essence of the characteristic temperament of this particular section of the Alps.

Compared with other towns in Italy or the Po Valley, the Piedmontese heritage is severe, with an indefinable "western" resonance that stems from the Alpine backdrop to their armory of spires and towers. Theirs is a different strain of the Italic spirit. During several centuries of ascendancy over Piedmont, the Savoy left the mark of their caste, a highland culture that had long tended toward withdrawal and an unwillingness to abandon its own area of identity. Later they did forsake their insularity, and took on the burdensome role of piloting the country's political unification; but despite adopting a more "Italian" identity, Piedmont has never lost its birthright of highland severity and uprightness, discernible to this day throughout the region.

The highland constitution also shows up in a general industriousness. It is no coincidence that Piedmont has always been one of the powerhouses of Italian industrialism—not so much for the region's supply of hydroelectric energy from the Alpine valleys as for the characteristic highland commitment of the men and women who built Piedmontese industry. Turin is known worldwide for its automobile manufacturing, Ivrea for its typewriters and electronic engineering, Biella for its position as the vanguard of textile production. Thanks to the inexorable spread of the manufacturing industries that have turned the entire west section of the valley beneath the Alps into a single, continuous industrial settlement — stretching from Biella and Turin to Ivrea and Pinerolo — Piedmont's urban texture is geared to production, often intense. The outcome is a blanket of recent land development, forming an unbroken periphery of expansion. The old Savoy nuclei abide, however, with their distinctive architecture accumulated over the seventeenth and eighteenth century and later enriched by architects working under the Savoy dynasty. Palatial residences, barracks, sanctuaries, and churches provide the cultural landmarks of a domain with a style of its own. The pinnacle of achievement in this direction is Turin, with its geometrical layout and orderliness, constructed ambitiously by the local monarchy in deference to the Enlightenment. Despite their highland extraction, the Savoys absorbed European culture as a whole, and particularly that from across the Alps, spanning the division between a Mediterranean country and advanced, preeminent Europe.

■ 9. A view of Turin that has virtually become a stereotype, taken from the Superga hillside across the Po river; from here the streets lead toward the regular geometries that confer order on the city. Many buildings in this area of Turin, like those facing onto Piazza Vittorio Veneto on the right, date from the eighteenth century. Soaring 167 meters above the city is the famous spire built by Alessandro Antonelli, rivaled only by the cupola of the duomo in the distance. In the background the snow-capped peaks of Mount Cozie and Mount Graie delimit the range of the Piedmont Alps.

■ 10. Left: Inside the cupola of the chapel which houses the Turin Shroud, in the cathedral of San Giovanni Battista. The cupola is the work of the seventeenth-century architect Guarino Guarini, one of the eminent draftsmen working under the Savoy family, who contributed greatly to the renovation of Turin's architectural heritage. This extraordinary example of baroque mastery is grafted onto the Renaissance cathedral, adding an ingenious note of diversity to the fifteenth-century masterpiece of the Tuscan artist Meo del Caprina.

■ 11. One of the buildings looking onto Piazza San Carlo, Turin's most neatly designed and monumental square. An example of Savoy architecture bestowing tone and nobility to the face of the city, the building's style is baroque, with inserts of neoclassicism — characteristic features such as frames, capitals, and pilaster strips — and decorative additions such as Savoy friezes and iconographic motifs. This kind of architecture, also found outside Turin in other towns throughout the region, was practiced mainly by architects active under the Savoy court throughout the seventeenth and eighteenth centuries, including Filippo Juvarra, the Castellamonte brothers, and Guarino Guarini, who produced works of great prestige.

■ 12. The stables of the Pinerolo military academy, an eminent Savoy institution originally sited in a village at the entrance to the Val Chisone, which offered a strategic vantage point for military purposes. Under French domination between the sixteenth and seventeenth century, the town's defense works were augmented with important fortifications designed by the renowned military architect De Vauban. The military academy was founded in the last century, and closed during World War II. The vast complex of buildings that originally housed the academy now houses an interesting museum with a collection of curios, uniforms, arms, harnesses, and other weaponry used by the once crucial military corps.

■ 13. A throng of people in Piazza Vittorio Emanuele (also known as Piazza Citt) in Ivrea celebrating the carnival festivities, one of the town's most heartfelt traditions. During the carnival various figures from the past are brought back to life to illustrate the town's history, starting from the age of communes. Ivrea passed into the hands of the Savoys in the fourteenth century and numbered among their prize possessions as the gateway to the Valle d'Aosta. Cradled in a natural amphitheater of hills known as the Serra, it is now an industrial town famous above all for being the home of the Olivetti company, founded here by a dynasty of enlightened entrepreneurs.

■ 14. The arcades of Cuneo's busy central Piazza Galimberti, a spacious square encircled by porticoed facades. This Piedmont town, situated on a terrace formed by the confluence of two valleys sloping down from the Maritime Alps and the Cozie Alps, was strategically important as a passage for transalpine traffic coming over the Tenda and Maddalena passes. Its growth is fairly recent, however, and the layout it received under the Savoys, with its baroque palaces and open, airy urban plan, has survived the developments of this century.

■ 15. A view of the baptistery of San Pietro, one of the most prominent medieval buildings of Asti. The town has a long history and boasts various important buildings from the age of the communes, such as the striking towers. The baptistery, also known as the Rotonda, is built on a central floorplan and surmounted by an octagonal lantern just visible here between the arches of the neighboring church of San Pietro di Conzavia, now a museum. The House of Savoy has not forgotten to leave its mark on the originally medieval town, as seen in certain aspects of the town plan and some of its baroque buildings.

■ 16. The basilica of Sant'Andrea, the pride of Vercelli and the symbol itself of this thriving town in Piedmont. Although its basic tone is a mixture of Romanesque and Gothic, this outstanding church seems to defy tradition with an imaginative order and authentic balance of its own. The two towers flanking the facade are strikingly unusual, if faithful to the Gothic cathedral scheme. The cuspidate belfry was erected a few centuries after the basilica. The use of terracotta, typical to Lombardy, is an intelligent interplay of mass and void, using mullioned windows with two and three lights, pilasters, and so forth. The basilica oversees a plain of rice fields, which create a series of breathtaking mirrors reflecting the cathedral and its twin towers when flooded in spring. During the Middle Ages, when much of the Po Valley was still uninhabited the marshes were gradually reclaimed by monks of the Cistercian order, who also saw to the building of Sant'Andrea, then part of their monastery, between the twelfth and thirteenth centuries.

■ 17. Right: The Arengario or town hall, the oldest of a group of medieval buildings called the Broletto in the heart of Novara. Situated at the easternmost boundary of Piedmont, Novara is the Piedmont town least affected by the Savoy legacy, having stronger ties with nearby Milan. Its position is important, as attested by its basically Roman layout. In the late Middle Ages Novara was a commune and passed successively into the duchies of the Visconti and the Sforza families before a lengthy domination by the Spanish and the progressive decline of the town. In the last century, Novara's town plan was radically reworked, with the Spanish walls torn down . This gave the town its eighteenth- and nineteenth-century tone while allowing its well- preserved medieval heirlooms to stand out, like this magnificent Arengario.

MILAN AND THE CITIES OF LOMBARDY.
The Mark of Prosperity

*T*he city of Milan lies at the center of a plain named after the ancient Longobardia, a region discovered by early Germanic populations who marveled at its lush green landscapes and rivers. The Romans called the city Mediolanum in deference to its position on an almost imperceptible line that divides the land into two plains of different importance, both demarcated by rivers. Milan has fulfilled a fundamental historical role as the center of a region that consolidated its identity over the centuries by means of the powerful dynasties that ruled over it, the Visconti and Sforza families. This legacy is manifest in the city's monuments and art treasures, which are often overlooked in favor of its other achievements.

Few other cities in Italy have been such an incubator of history and culture as Milan, generating trade, handicrafts, and industries of all kinds. Toward the end of the last century when the country finally achieved political unification, Milan showed its prowess as the leader of the entire national economy, imposing its financial, business, and cultural supremacy on the rest of the country while appropriating European influences in a highly original and supremely Italian way. For a long time the city bore the title of "moral capital" of the nation, due to the upright mores of its middle-class population. Today, this once proud, energetic, original, and creative city has lost some of its luster, but it is still at the helm of new developments in the north of Italy, home of most of the country's service-sector industries spread over most of the complex grid of urban development stretching from Piedmont to Veneto.

In its growth, which is not always entirely felicitous, Lombardy's metropolis has erased a sizable quota of the region's history. Formerly, small and medium-sized towns were evenly scattered over the region, their belfries visible over the tops of the tree plantations which still grace the countryside. In many cases these towns have managed to preserve their structure, especially those in the lower plain, less affected by the recent process of urban and industrial development: Lodi, Crema, Cremona, Pavia, and Vigevano have more or less been spared, not to mention Mantua, which has kept its integrity, having been the capital of the state of the Gonzaga dynasty. For centuries, the towns of Lombardy developed in close harmony with the rest of the plain, acquiring their character from their intimate ties with the surrounding countryside and populating the horizons of the Po Valley with brick churches and palazzi in an unmistakable architectural style that blends with the rivers, the trees, and the land of Lombardy. The towns in the lower plain, though set among rivers, rice fields, and irrigation canals, are somewhat different from those in the upper part of the Po Valley. Certain towns in the Alpine foothills, such as Bergamo, Brescia, and Como (the latter two built on an original Roman street plan), were under Venetian dominion: with the valleys behind them, they served as bridges between the plain and the mountains. Despite their links with Milan these towns continue as capitals of longstanding industrialized areas, enjoying intense economic activity and the rapid urban expansion which snakes into the valleys beyond. But the antiquity and nobility of their history lies in the charm of the monuments in the old town centers. Bergamo is the most evocative and intact; perched high on the crest of a hill, it seems to look out with venerable dismay over the devastated plain below.

■ 18. A view of Milan against the Alpine foothills of Lombardy. The zoom lens makes them look far closer than they are. Milan does have its days of clear skies ("such a beautiful sky, in beautiful weather," wrote the local novelist Alessandro Manzoni), when the foehn, a warm dry wind, sweeps away the foul and often polluted city air. Such clear days reveal just how extraordinary Milan's location is, with the band of

Alpine foothills to the north, Monte Rosa and the Alps of Piedmont to the northwest, and the Apennines to the south. The favorable position of Lombardy's metropolis between the upper and lower plain, on the main routes linking the transalpine passes with the Po Valley and the Apennines, has largely determined its good fortune and its uninterrupted primacy, as witnessed by its ample legacy of historical buildings. Considered the most authentically European of Italy's cities, Milan is not only a major economic and commercial focus but also the leader of the country's finance, industry, and culture. But although it is the main focus of the service sector, Milan has still not responded adequately to the necessary growth of modern service functions. It has not even attempted to renovate its appearance; the few skyscrapers which animate the skyline were built in the 1960s when the city experienced a mighty explosion in population and productive activity. As with other cities, Milan is trying to reorganize and streamline itself but in the process is losing much of its essential character. All the same the city remains a leader, grasping and tackling its problems ahead of other cities throughout the country.

■ 19 & 20. Two views of Milan's cathedral: on the left, the apse, and on the right, the roof in the snow. This magnificent house of worship is considered to be the symbol of the city. Like all fine churches and cathedrals, the Duomo is not only an expression of the ambitions of the townsfolk or religious hierarchy, but also of the city's economic possibilities.

The cathedral is a complex building. Due to this complexity and the never-ending repairs it has required over the years, the building has never really been completed. Though it does not rank high in Italian architectural history, it is certainly an extraordinary work of art. It is also one of the country's best-known monuments thanks to its sheer size and to the wealth and intricacy of the detailing, sculpted in pale Candoglia marble brought from the nearby Alpine foothills. Construction work on the Duomo began in 1386 under the dominion of the Visconti family. Its pointed facade, one of many designs presented, is quite incongruous to its Gothic form and was added in more recent times. A forest of pinnacles crown the building, and at the back, the soaring main spire bears a gold-plated statue of the Virgin Mary.

From her lofty perch 108 meters above the city the Madonnina or "little madonna" looks protectively on her flock below.

■ 21 & 22. Overleaf, left: The towers of the Sforza Castle. This imposing stronghold dominates the fabric of Milan's downtown, looking down Via Dante, one of the main streets to the Duomo. Just as the Duomo was once a token of religious strength, the castle symbolized political power. The form it has today is modeled on the original built by the powerful Sforza dynasty, which governed the Duchy of Milan through the fifteenth and sixteenth centuries. Completed around the year 1496, the castle's master builders and artists included Filarete and Jacopo da Cortona. Today it houses museums and libraries. Right: The Naviglio Grande, a canal constructed during the twelfth century. Fed by the Ticino river from almost fifty kilometers away, the canal crosses the western plain of Lombardy and penetrates deep into Milan. At one time the entire city was networked by navigable canals, linking the city center with the extensive system of waterways crossing the Lombardy plain. In the course of this century many canals were covered over, depriving Milan of one of its most intriguing assets. This part of the Naviglio has nevertheless remained intact, and its iron footbridges are a token of the city's intense industrial background.

■ 23. The famous Piazza Ducale in Vigevano, viewed from the splendid arcade running round its perimeter. Towering over the square is Bramante's castle tower, with its remarkable tapering form. The castle and square, set in the medieval burg, are a brilliant Renaissance creation supposedly commissioned by Ludovico il Moro to Leonardo da Vinci. The construction of the square, which served as access to the castle, dated back to 1492–94. All the buildings are brick, adorned with highly-prized decorative work.

■ 24. A different view of Piazza Ducale, the heart of Vigevano, a kind of open-air salon or foyer. Immediately welcoming, the piazza is a superb venture in creating a harmonious setting scaled to human values. The scheme's strength lies in providing Vigevano with a square that is at once a historical and sentimental focus. The town is a prosperous one, relatively independent notwithstanding the overall potency of nearby Milan; its main resource lies in shoe manufacturing. Thankfully, the square is out-of-bounds to motor vehicles.

■ 25. The Ponte Coperto over the Ticino river at Pavia. This covered bridge, first constructed in the fourteenth century, is one of the main historical attractions of the town. The current bridge is a reconstruction of the original, which was destroyed by bombing during World War II and had two roofs and a drawbridge at either end. The roof was not much different, however, and was supported by a series of small columns built in the sixteenth century. Pavia's ties with the Ponte Coperto are part and parcel of those with the river flowing through it, which gives the town its character.

■ 26. Right: The Belcredi tower and the San Dalmazzo tower, two medieval structures dominating the town center of Pavia. These and towers like them give a decidedly medieval look to the town (regrettably, in 1989 the civic tower collapsed). Throughout the Middle Ages, Pavia achieved prominence first as the seat of the Longobard kings and capital of their *Regnum Italicum* (from the sixth to the ninth century) and later as a free commune. Some of the fine churches ennobling Pavia's town center date back to the medieval period. The old part of the town follows the street plan of its Roman precursor, *Ticinum*, which had its center near the cathedral. Home of one of Italy's most venerable universities, founded in the fourteenth century, Pavia is situated in a busy industrial and agricultural area.

■ 27. Overleaf: Piazza della Vittoria, Lodi, one of the finest squares in Lombardy, renowned for its surrounding arcades and the beautiful facade of the Duomo, which looks out across the cobbled paving — a reminder of when the streets and squares of towns throughout the Po Valley were made of stone and not asphalt. The grandeur of this spacious central public square is representative of the town's rich legacy from the era of the free communes and the times of Milanese domination. The wealth of the agricultural land, irrigated by the Adda river, also contributes to the noble aspect of this town in southern Lombardy.

■ 28. A view of Como, cradled in the western extremity of the lake of the same name. More recent developments are visible around the old town center, and others on the overhang slopes of the Alpine foothills. Como's Gothic-Renaissance cathedral is one of the most interesting religious buildings in Lombardy and was built in the fourteenth century on the remains of a late medieval basilica. It is located in the heart of the town, where the street plan follows the original orthogonal layout of the Roman *Comum*. From its position at the end of the lake, Como has always mediated between the plains of Lombardy and the lake valleys and transalpine passes, prospering as the capital of Italy's silk industry.

29. The Broletto, an ancient palazzo in the cathedral square in Como. The building dates back to the early thirteenth century and was partly renovated in the fifteenth century. Together with the Duomo, the Broletto is a token of the history of this town, which was a thriving commune before passing to the duchy of Milan during the era of the seignories.

■ 30. Left: The main gateway into the cathedral square, Crema. This seventeenth-century gateway is part of a monumental group, with the town hall and the Torrazzo, which ennobles this authentically Lombard town. Crema's striking streets and buildings are typical of the Po region, a mixture of rural liveliness and moments of quiet, during which the scent of the countryside seems to waft into the heart of town. Its oldest buildings date from the times of the free commune, but many others were built during the domination of the Venetian republic, which explains the bas-relief of the Lion of San Marco over the arch of this gateway.

■ 31. A rather unusual winter scene in Piazza Vecchia in old Bergamo, site of the town's most significant historical monuments. In the background is Palazzo Nuovo, an elegant edifice in Palladian style begun in the sixteenth century by Vallone and later modified by Vincenzo Scamozzi. The building currently houses the municipal library.

■ 32. Overleaf: A view of Bergamo Alta, the original nucleus of the town, where a ring of nineteenth-century houses encloses the ancient towers, together with belfries and domes of the cathedral and Santa Maria Maggiore. Also visible is the part of the perimeter wall enclosing the old town, which sits on the crest of a hill overlooking the lower city below and out across the plain. The dual character of Bergamo, split between the upper section of town and the rest below, on the one hand denotes the historic old burg on its high perch like an Alpine sentry, and on the other the dynamic modern township mediating between the plain and the mountainside, between the metropolis of Milan and the suburban territories, between the people of the valley and those of the Alpine foothills.

■ 33. The little market in the shadow of the Loggia, one of the most eminent buildings of Brescia's historical center. This Renaissance building was conceived at the end of the fifteenth century by Filippo De Grassi and completed in the second half of the sixteenth by the most prominent architects operating in the Venetian Republic, including Sansovino and Palladio. Together with other outstanding monuments, the Loggia is emblematic of the prosperous background of the city, well located amidst the lively valley industries and the fertile farmlands in the plain.

■ 34. Right: Another view of Brescia, this time of the Rotonda, otherwise known as the old Duomo, now part of the new cathedral, which is just out of view. This church, erected in the eleventh century on a sixth- to seventh-century early Christian basilica, is most representative of Brescia's medieval heritage, marking a period in which the town began to grow on the foundations of the earlier Roman settlement. The name Rotonda refers to the circular structure visible here, with its splendid walls encircling a church with a central floorplan.

■ 35. Cremona: The beautiful facade of the Duomo on Piazza del Comune, in the heart of the town. On the right side of the square stands the baptistery and, next to the Duomo, the Torrazzo, a tall bell-tower which gives the town its unmistakable and almost magical character. The Duomo is one of the finest in the Po Valley, which boasts many magnificent cathedrals. Its construction dates back to the twelfth century, though it underwent alterations during the fifteenth and sixteenth centuries. The beauty of the Duomo and the appeal of the square have endured admirably through time; thanks to the town's provincial character and agricultural economy, its local Po Valley character has been left undisturbed.

■ 36 & 37. Overleaf, left: The Teatro Antico, Sabbioneta. This small town in the Mantua area is styled around the urban tastes of Vespasiano Gonzaga and his family. During the second half of the sixteenth century, Vespasiano decided he wanted to make Sabbioneta a "little Athens." The town's Renaissance layout and buildings embody an ideal town plan, a kind of urban utopia. The theater was designed by Vincenzo Scamozzi and is reminiscent of Palladio's famous Teatro Olimpico in Vicenza. Right: The arcades of the Palazzo Ducale in Mantua. The palazzo looks onto Piazza Sordello, together with some of the city's main historical buildings. These alone give a clear idea of the opulence of the Gonzaga state, which, while not of any great size, prided itself for an abundance of culture, enterprise, and illuminated minds. The Palazzo Ducale was the royal palace of the city's dukes; today it houses an outstanding museum, which gives an excellent portrait of the artistic and cultural activities in the courts of the smaller Italian states during the Renaissance.

THE CITIES OF EMILIA-ROMAGNA. One Long *Decumanum*

*T*he pattern of urban growth in Emilia-Romagna is one of the most curious in Europe, a long series of towns along the Via Emilia, a consistently straight road following the original causeway built by the Romans in the first century A.D. to join the Po Valley and transalpine roads to Rimini on the Adriatic coast. Rimini was the terminus of the main northbound causeway, the Via Salaria, which led up through the Apennines from Rome. The Via Emilia runs along the northern edge of the Apennines, punctuated by a town at each junction of the Via Emilia with other roads from the hillside. The resulting pattern adapts the human organization of the territory to the natural order of the land, merging human and physical geography. From Rimini the road leads to Cesena, Forlì, Faenza, Imola, Bologna, Modena, Reggio Emilia, Parma, and Piacenza.

The extent of each town's development is geared to the importance of the Apennine valley with which it corresponds. All the towns, however, are focused on the old causeway, which acts as one long decumanum (the main street that ran lengthwise through the towns of the Romans). Consequently, most of Emilia-Romagna's towns have the same basic pattern. Their historical town centers, often based on the original Roman grid, are clustered round the Via Emilia, which serves as the main street through each town, providing a backbone for the urban fabric. This core is usually made up of old buildings, mostly in brick, of a light, golden-brown color, distinct from the dark reddish tone of the brick used in Lombardy. This golden-brown is the color of Emilia. Another shared feature of Emilia-Romagna's towns is the running ground-floor arcades on either side of the street. These covered walkways provide a continuous space for meeting, strolling, and pausing outside the shops. Here too is an abundance of fine Romanesque churches and magnificent piazzas.

Today the towns of Emilia-Romagna have extended from the old center toward the railway line running parallel with the Via Emilia, and from there to the Bologna-Rimini motorway, which has attracted factories and housing developments. These three lines of communication — the Roman decumanum, the railway, and the motorway — demarcate different eras of urban development.

But there are other kinds of urban formation in the region of Emilia-Romagna. Near the Po river we find Ferrara, a town quite unlike any other. Once capital of the Este duchy, Ferrara has many original assets, not least its town plan, designed in the sixteenth century by Biagio Rossetti. A more recent kind of development can be found along the coast in the seaside resorts. Here the main historical attraction is Ravenna, the former Byzantine capital, late-medieval in style. After years of development, the coastline is one unbroken chain of hotels, residences, boardinghouses and campsites, which cater to a summer population of several million — the vacationers' "metropolis," the summer venue for unbridled spending and wild entertainment. Hardly restful, the entire area reverberates with the noise of vacationers and suffers from misuse of both sea and land. The eye of the storm here is Rimini, originally a Roman settlement; but, given the patterns of development, it is impossible to tell where one town leaves off and the next one starts. Here too, nevertheless, the old causeway, the railway line, and the motorway delimit successive phases of urban growth.

■ 38. One of the equestrian statues dominating Piazza dei Cavalli, the historical and topographical center of Piacenza. The statues were made in the seventeenth century by Francesco Mochi to celebrate the Farnese princes who governed the town from the mid-sixteenth to eighteenth century, during Papal dominion. In the background, the thirteenth-century facade of San Francesco in Lombard gothic style. The most westerly of towns along the Roman Via Emilia, Piacenza also has a geometric street plan, based on the Roman quadrilateral and amplified during the Middle Ages.

■ 39. Inside the dome of the baptistery in Parma. This building, which stands alongside the cathedral, is among the town's finest monuments and has been defined by art historians as the "most unified and coherent monument from the period of transition from Romanesque to Gothic." The detailing is the work of Benedetto Antelami, an artist who mixed his styles and is responsible for the outstanding sculptures in the lunettes over the doorways and for the high reliefs depicting the months of the year. The frescoes decorating the dome, mainly from the thirteenth century, are also admirably executed and represent episodes from the Bible and various evangelical figures.

■ 40. A view across the cathedral square in Parma. Thanks to the cathedral and the baptistery on two of its sides, the square is one of Italy's most enchanting. The cathedral itself is a magnificent example of Romanesque architecture, adorned with a series of small galleries, portals, and a portico over the central doorway. Its construction dates from the twelfth century (though it existed earlier in a different form), and hence it predates the baptistery. Slightly removed from the busy town center, the square has a rather arcane atmosphere in which one can grasp the individuality of the Po Valley towns, with their long heritage of urban culture.

■ 41. A view of the city center of Reggio Emilia, down the street that leads to Piazza Cesare Battisti. One can just glimpse part of the eighteenth-century town hall. The dome of the cathedral is also visible in the background. Reggio Emilia's historical core is clustered around the Via Emilia, which cuts through it from east to west. The city's thriving economy is based on industry and farming.

■ 42. Right: The rose window of the exquisitely harmonious facade of Modena cathedral. This house of worship, unanimously considered to be the finest example of Romanesque art in Italy, was built in the twelfth century by master-builders from Como, including Anselmo da Campione, who designed the rose window, and Wiligelmo, author of the bas-reliefs and sculptures adorning the facade and portals.

■ 43 & 44. Overleaf: Two impressions of Bologna, the largest and most populous city along the Via Emilia. Left: The statue of Neptune near Piazza Maggiore, the symbolic and geometrical center of the city. The bronzes are the work of Giambologna and date from 1566. The rest of the fountain was designed by Tomaso Laureti. Behind it stands Palazzo Re Enzo and the belfry of the Duomo. Right: A view of the city center from the top of the Garisenda tower (forty-eight meters high), showing the streets running east to west parallel to the Via Emilia on the right. In the foreground, the domes of San Bartolomeo. The even rows of roofs are tiled in terracotta, a material found everywhere in Bologna. The city's old center is among the country's most thoughtfully preserved.

■ 45. Piazza Trento e Trieste in Ferrara, showing the right flank of the cathedral. Despite its jumble of modifications, mostly made in the eighteenth century, the cathedral is one of the most significant medieval monuments in Italy. Its tiers of arches were created by Como craftsmen between the twelfth and fourteenth centuries. One curious feature is the gallery, dubbed the Loggia dei Merciai, comprising a series of merchants' booths set along the side of the cathedral in the fifteenth century. Behind the piazza one can just glimpse the town hall, originally the residence of the Este family.

■ 46. The bases of the towers of the massive Este fortress in the heart of Ferrara. This imposing brick construction surrounded by a moat is a vivid expression of the power of the dukes of Este, the dynasty that ruled over Ferrara from the thirteenth to the sixteenth century, and which, by means of acute trade policies and cultural commitment, turned Ferrara into a thriving city. The closeness of the Po river was clearly a key factor in the development of both the duchy and the growing town, but the enterprising spirit of the Estes and the local bourgeoisie (mostly of Jewish origin) was fundamental. Witness the splendid buildings of the fifteenth and sixteenth century, the period of Ferrara's greatest glory, and the highly innovative urban plan, the *Addizione Erculea*, named after Ercole d'Este, the man who commissioned the work to the architect and town planner Biagio Rossetti.

■ 47. The Malatesta library, a Renaissance institution of vital importance in the Romagnola town of Cesena. The library communicates a strong humanist sense of purpose and a meditative feeling of the past centuries. Built in the second half of the fifteenth century as a convent library, though it later passed into municipal jurisdiction, it was administered by monks until the last century. Its rare collections include some priceless fifteenth-century codices in Latin, Greek, and Hebrew as well as many precious miniated volumes (among others, a thirteenth-century Bible and Saint Augustine's *De Civitate*). The building itself is based on a basilican plan with three aisles and an elegant row of columns, as seen here.

■ 48. Right: The basilica of San Vitale in the town of Ravenna. This house of worship is one of the town's most prized monuments, and an extraordinary example of the Byzantine art that prospered along the Adriatic coast during the era in which oriental Christian culture encountered western Roman culture. The building has an octagonal plan and a central dome. Although following Roman canons for its shape, the building betrays oriental influences in the lavishness of its decorations, the emphasis on the central dome, and the exploitation of the effects of light and shade. The mosaics of the apse shown in the photograph depict Christ and various saints. The basilica, built toward the middle of the sixth century, is one of several Byzantine buildings of the unique heritage of Ravenna, whose influence as a center of culture and religious life spread through the Adriatic, and to Venice in particular.

■ 49. Piazza del Popolo in the heart of Faenza, with its magnificent fountain in the foreground and the surrounding arcaded frontage. The view gives an immediate idea of the acute civil sense pervading this town, famous throughout the world since the Middle Ages for its fine ceramics. The oldest examples of faience date as far back as 1142, and a series of statutes regulating production were drafted shortly after. Faenza's ceramics were appreciated as far away as China itself. Today the city celebrates its heritage with a museum and various signal works of architecture (some medieval), and a sublime cathedral in Renaissance style.

■ 50. Ferrara: Street signage dating from the start of the century. The importance of the towns along the Po river is always rooted in their history. When Italy achieved political unification in the last century, they became provincial capitals, and their duties and importance increased. The provinces, however, teem with smaller towns of considerable historical interest, spread out across the land in more or less the same pattern defined centuries ago. According to the hierarchy established by the Unification, the old signage has continued to favor the provincial capitals.

THE RIVIERA CITIES OF LIGURIA AND TUSCANY.
Port Activity and Tourism

*A*long the coastline that stretches from the Ligurian to the Tyrrhenian Sea lies a chain of towns whose distinctive nature is largely determined by their indelible links with the sea. Most are squeezed into a narrow strip of land below the steep mountain range commanding the coast, where here and there the inhospitable crags give way to brief sandy bays at the foot of narrow gorges in the mountains, usually the site of a village or town. The geographical conformation has left the Ligurian interior sparsely inhabited and ill-equipped to nourish the area's towns. Wherever the coastal settlement was able to link up with a more dynamic interior, a major port or city evolved — as with Genoa, which has been the main seaport of Italy's richest and most industrialized region for over a century. Other towns which followed this pattern were Imperia and Savona, and — in more recent history — La Spezia, which used to be a crucial military port, and Leghorn. The latter became Tuscany's main port when the harbor of Pisa, which throughout the Middle Ages had shared the control of the upper Tyrrhenian Sea with Genoa, became unusable because of extensive silting.

From the very outset, Genoa's fortunes have stemmed from its role as a seaport. Despite the lack of space, this extraordinary city gradually crept up the mountainsides encircling its artificial port. Genoa's development as a city commenced in the Middle Ages, when it was an important marine republic. Its trading skills accompanied it through successive centuries, facilitated by its expansion operations overseas and an innate talent for navigation which earned it a leading role in the history of Europe. Late last century, Genoa teamed its marine activities with those of industry, such as the processing of imported mineral products. Despite the many problems involved, this combination has continued to be Genoa's forte throughout this century.

In the meantime, however, Leghorn and La Spezia have come to rival Genoa in size and importance. The development of other centers along the coast is a more recent affair, due to the burgeoning tourist exploitation of the Riviera. With their mild climate, the coastal resorts have drawn increasing crowds of vacationers over the century, especially northern Italians. Tourism has consequently given rise to "garden cities," towns made up entirely of villas, boardinghouses, and hotels, like Sanremo. Elsewhere along the western and eastern stretches of the Riviera, however, villages and towns fell prey to building speculators (often proceeding without authorization). Today, these areas are besieged by masses of concrete that often make it virtually impossible to enjoy the seaside. In many cases the ancient town centers, which had links with both sea and land with their marine and horticultural activities, have been destroyed by the invasion of concrete.

The Tyrrhenian Sea washes against that splendid stretch of coast around Viareggio, known as Versilia — climatically ideal because it is screened from the north winds by the Apuan Alps in much the same way that Liguria is protected by its Alps and the Apennines. But unlike the Ligurian Riviera Versilia boasts vast sandy shores, which have always attracted throngs of vacationers. Its popularity has given rise to an unbroken chain of resorts, almost one long coastal city (similar to development along the Adriatic coastline of Emilia-Romagna). The main town on this strip of development from La Spezia to Leghorn, Viareggio is a concentration of the coast's characteristics. Originally the home of boatmen and sailors, at the end of the last century Viareggio became a focus of hotels, luxury villas, and residences forming a distillation of the history of Italian seaside resorts and the developing tastes and fashions of the local middle class, as well as typifying the kind of town planning generated in Italy by the rites and rituals of summer vacationing.

■ 51. Genoa's historical downtown, with its concentration of buildings, churches, bell towers, and domes and, in the distance, the old port. This medieval nucleus has two important features. The first is the antiquity of the urban fabric and the sheer beauty of its monuments (such as the unusual banded belfry of San Lorenzo). The second is the way in which Genoa is crammed into a tight space, huddled over the old port, from which the city derives its strength and uniqueness. The modern part of the city has gradually sought space on the surrounding hillsides; consequently the new harbor, like the old port, was created with infill and the complex of docks and shipping plants were progressively built out into the water. With modernization, however, the medieval core of the city has been badly neglected.

■ 52. Overleaf: Funicular railway linking the lower section of the city with the higher Righi district, a new residential area with an excellent view of the city. The limited space available in the central core of the town has forced Genoa to expand up the neighboring mountain slopes, giving today's city its singular, "climbing" form of large buildings constructed up the hillside, often ingeniously poised to great scenic effect.

■ 53. On the preceding page: The towers and belfries of Albenga. This town lies on the widest coastal strip of the western Riviera. Since classical times this extra space has made it an important agricultural center as well as a busy port. Of pre-Roman foundation, the town's origins lie with the Ingauni tribes; later it became the Roman seaport of *Albingaunum*. In the early Middle Ages it was the seat of government under the Franks and subsequently a free commune, as it remained until the fifteenth century, albeit under various forms of domination. The town's monuments, dating from the times of the communes, include the municipal tower and numerous other towers built by the various dominating families of the times, and the beautiful, twelfth-century cathedral of San Michele; the famous baptistery dates back to the fifth century.

■ 54. A glimpse of the industrial plants in Piombino, midway along the Maremma coastline and still one of the main centers of the Italian steel industry. The modern iron and steel industry developed in Piombino for the same reasons that guided the Etruscans to choose nearby *Populonia* as a center for working iron ore brought onshore from Elba. Piombino itself grew around this kind of activity. Later, particularly during Fascism and World War II, Piombino boosted its output by utilizing imported minerals, allying itself with Italy's other capitals of the iron and steel industry.

■ 55. Right: Old houses in Leghorn, whose urban history is quite unlike any other in Tuscany. Leghorn's development is essentially "modern," and dates back to the sixteenth century. Its fortunes began when the Granduchy of Tuscany chose it to be a harbor outlet after the port of Pisa was filled in. A manmade canal was then built linking Leghorn to the Arno river. The town has continued to grow in consequence over the years, particularly in more recent times as it has become a major port for the thriving industrial interior. The city still has an antiquated look, with its old houses, fortifications, and canals branching off from the port.

■ 56. A shipyard for fishing-boat construction in Savona. The town's marine tradition goes back far into the past. Although overshadowed by Genoa, Savona has not lost its prominence as a seaport and natural terminus for the main roads leading over the Apennines from the Po Valley. Today Savona continues to serve as a port, and has recently increased operations with the construction of an oil-processing port, with vast thermoelectric and raw-material processing plants. The tower in the background is a reminder of the town's distant medieval beginnings.

■ 57. Figureheads from old ships and sailboats at the Museo Tecnico Navale in the Military Arsenal at La Spezia. The museum also offers a collection of vessels, nautical instruments, weapons from old warships, antique nautical maps and papers, and other items which narrate the glorious history of the Italian Navy. Ever since the early days of Savoy dominion La Spezia has been an important military base. Today the port is in constant expansion and handles a heavy traffic of mainly imported goods.

■ 58. Left: A typical, Liberty-style building in Viareggio — a reminder of the early days of tourism. This style of building gave Viareggio its peculiar tone, evocative of an earlier Italy dominated by a stubbornly elitist middle class composed of industrialists and wealthy landowners who lived out their worldly social rites in towns like Viareggio. Despite their parochial leanings, they were open to influences and fashions from Europe and beyond. Like other holiday resorts on the Ligurian and Adriatic coasts, Viareggio was the setting for the disillusionment of provincial (and still largely rural) Italy in the late nineteenth and early twentieth century.

■ 59. A glimpse of Cagliari from the sea. The ancient center of the Sardinian capital is both Mediterranean and southern Italian through and through. It has some of the urban flair of Naples, and its port has provided new and unique openings for the island, which has always otherwise been cloistered and inward-looking in its pastoral and archaic culture. Cagliari is also the largest city on the island, fulfilling the role of mediator between Sardinia and a mainland which is not quite so remote as in earlier days. Yet, substantially, the island's relationship with the mainland is one of passive dependence.

THE CITIES OF THE VENETO. Breezes from the Foothills and the Lagoon

Veneto (or Venetia) is a region of outstanding beauty lying between the Alps and the sea. Its most vital area is the part of the plain which extends from the Alpine foothills to the lagoons on the Adriatic. Large or small, the towns of this part of the region — such as Padua, Treviso, Bassano, and Vicenza — are steeped in history. Further west lies Verona; while also belonging to Veneto, it enjoys a certain amount of autonomy due to links beyond the Adige river to the Alps and the reaches of Lombardy.

The towns of the Veneto have all played a prominent role in Italy's history, from Roman times to the Middle Ages, and thence from the period of the free communes through the Renaissance and on to the seventeenth century. None, however, escaped the influence of the lagoon city Venice, capital of a dominion that began in the fifteenth century when the city began to extend its hegemony inland after years of primacy on the seas. As a consequence, each of Veneto's towns bears the hallmark of Venice, a kind of extension inland of the city's glorious vision. Venice is utterly unique. The image it has created of itself is one that plays eternally in the waters of the lagoon. Its architecture reflects the magic and fortune of a mighty, affluent city, assertive in its trading, wise in its administration of the republic, and enlightened in its pursuit of knowledge. The city's beauty and originality stem from a deep feeling for culture and an uncommon grasp of history. The main contributors to the history of the lagoon and its region were first the nobles, who became catalysts to the development of a cultural heritage that lives on in the glorious palazzi along the Canal Grande, and in the churches that give an inimitable look to Venice, a city where all religious feeling has been paganized by the force of historical disillusionment.

The noble facade of today's Venice, however, conceals a sense of emptiness. Besieged year-round by tourists, Venice has failed to keep abreast with the times. The industrial suburb, though set away from the main city, pollutes its waters and fouls its atmosphere. Industrialization in the region is typified by Porto Marghera on the neighboring mainland, one of a host of industrial centers which continue to spread northward toward the Alps, stretching from Mestre to Padua, from Treviso to Bassano, from Vicenza to Verona. Economic growth in Veneto has been almost exhaustive. Development is anarchic, littering the hillsides with concrete factories and characterless housing blocks. The irreparable damage inflicted on the countryside and the utter anonymity of this growth, however, are offset by the beauty and grace of the historical town centers. Treviso and Vicenza, with their noble squares and palaces, epitomize a vision of urban development tailored to human needs. The city of Padua, though relatively small in size, has a rich cultural background, championed by its historic university. Verona, with its river and its close bonds with both plain and hills, boasts relics from every era of history. Here as elsewhere throughout the region, the palazzi and churches endow town centers with the characteristic hallmark of Venice, its architecture successfully translated to an inland setting.

■ 60. The charm of Venice lies in its peerless architecture. Each alley, each canal, offers a new scenario, quite different from the one before. The lacework of the typical Venetian Gothic style provides a leitmotif throughout the city, emphasizing the exquisite marriage of marble and water, the union of the evanescent horizontals of the lagoon and the strong verticals of the architecture. Beyond the rows of gondolas looms the Palazzo Ducale, the archetype of the Venetian Gothic and symbol of the might of the Republic. Together with the basilica of San Marco, the palace is historically the most significant building in Venice, built over the fourteenth and fifteenth centuries when the republic had turned its sights on the mainland. Originally the residence of the Doges of the republic, the palace today is a museum for temporary exhibitions.

■ 61. The Canal Grande in Venice. Each
season in Venice has its own way of
exalting the extraordinary union of
water and architecture. The city's appeal
lies in the variety of forms offered by
the palazzi lining the canals, particularly
along the Canal Grande, an aquatic main
street with a rich display of aristocratic
architecture. It also lies in the colors of
the buildings themselves, here an array
of reds reflected on the water's surface.

■ 62. A view of the interior of San Marco (Saint Mark's), Venice's main house of worship. Built in the first half of the ninth century and successively reconstructed in the eleventh century, the basilica follows the typical Byzantine central plan; its embellishments are quite unique, however, with marble brought from all over the world, mosaics, bas-reliefs, sculptures, and paintings. The basilica is also a treasury of memories and reminders of the city's glorious history as a sea power. The interior is freighted with oriental designs evocative of profane mysteries, distant times, and far-off lands.

■ 63. An arcaded street in Treviso. Like nearby Padua, Treviso abounds with arcades, which help divide the distinct areas in which the town's daily life unfolds. Treviso has other important urban assets, such as Piazza dei Signori, the church of San Nicolò and the cathedral, and the so-called Palazzo del Trecento. The Venetian influence combines the nobility of the townscape with the inherent outgoing nature of its people, transforming the town into an ample and vivacious "salotto" or salon.

■ 64. Right: Donatello's famous equestrian statue in Padua of the Venetian condottiere, Gattamelata. The city boasts an ancient university of world fame, a wealth of valuable monuments and a rich artistic heritage. It also retains that distinct Veneto flair of living in harmony with the past, with the burden of culture and history, and the university is therefore part and parcel of daily life in Padua. Another important attraction is the basilica of Sant'Antonio, an important destination for pilgrimages, and — in a totally different vein — the site of the annual fair, an apt occasion for modern Padua, a busy economic and industrial center in the Veneto triangle.

■ 65. Bridges over the Canale della Vena, Chioggia. This town in the Venetian lagoon area is a fascinating smaller version of Venice. Despite emulating its powerful neighbor, Chioggia has remained aloof from Venice's ventures and exploits. Essentially provincial, it is still home to its population, as indeed the "campi" or squares of Venice were in the past. Thus the little town, with its fascinating canalside scenery and magnificent Duomo, is a real pleasure to visit. The local economy is based on fishing, and Chioggia ranks among Italy's major fishing centers.

■ 66. Right: The string of towers along the fortified walls of Montagnana, one of Italy's finest examples of fortified medieval towns, still structurally intact. These are in fact the original walls erected in the twelfth century by order of Ezzelino da Romano to defend the town, then the property of Padua, in response to the fortification of Legnago, near Verona. Inside, the urban fabric follows the geometrical structure of the perimeter walls, with a main street down the middle, bisected midway by a second street, creating a splendid square dominated by the Duomo at the very heart of the town.

■ 67. Overleaf: Sets for opera performances at Verona's world-famous arena. The most astonishing thing about the city's symbol-monument is that it is still being used in the same way as it was two thousand years ago — for staging popular events. In Roman times the arena was used for gladiator contests, and in later years for bullfights and football matches (Goethe described one of these matches in his book *Journey to Italy*, 1817). Today it is the celebrated venue of Verona's opera season. The original arena looked different from today's; its additional outer wall has since collapsed. The remaining structure is imposing, and seats up to twenty thousand spectators.

■ 68 & 69. Two scenes of Verona. Left: Piazza delle Erbe in the heart of the old town center, near the intersection of the two main streets of the Roman town, the *cardum* and the *decumanum*. This square, with its covered stalls of fruit, sweets, and souvenirs — traditionally the meeting point of the common townsfolk and gossips — is neatly contrasted to Piazza dei Signori, the venue of the town's gentry. Some of the buildings around this square are decorated with modern frescoes. Right: The Adige, which describes a broad loop round the old town, just visible on the right, with the imposing basilica of Sant'Anastasia. Beyond the river lies the "Veronetta," or little Verona, a medieval and more modern addition to the city. The bridge in the foreground is the exact replica of the Roman original destroyed during an air raid in World War II.

■ 70. Left: One of the most impressive works of the sixteenth-century architect Andrea Palladio, the basilica of Vicenza rises proudly above the old town center. The extraordinary legacy of Palladio's genius can be admired throughout the entire region. His work is representative of a deep relationship between Veneto's towns and their environs, a relationship in which urban art and tastes are introduced to the landscape and the town is permeated by a sense of the countryside. The main tower in the square is shown here, together with several other buildings, but it is Vicenza's heritage of noble palazzi which are responsible for making the entire town into a single, united "salotto" or salon for its inhabitants.

■ 71. The gallery of Udine's town hall (also known as the Loggia), a fine example of Venetian Gothic style. The old town center of Udine, capital of the Friuli region, boasts various buildings of considerable historic importance which attest to its eventful past, with that same urban sense encountered in many towns at the foot of the Veneto section of the Alps. But Udine is also very representative of Friuli itself, a dynamic region of great originality whose traditions and culture are manifest in its inhabitants and in the scenery of foothills and Alpine peaks.

THE CITIES OF TUSCANY. Hearts of "Italian Civilization"

*T*he towns and cities of Tuscany are among the country's most picturesque, due to the excellent state of preservation of their old centers and because they form a living testament to an era vital to the history of Italy, which lasted from the twelfth to the fifteenth century. Focuses of the most elaborate and refined of civil histories, these towns still offer sustained glimpses of the grace of a bygone era. Florence, perhaps the first city that springs to mind, is certainly the flagship of Tuscan urban culture; but other towns are equally fascinating, such as Siena, Pisa, Lucca, Pistoia, Prato, and Arezzo, not to mention smaller centers like San Gimignano, deep in the Tuscan hillside, defying change.

The appeal of the Tuscan towns is not only due to their architecture and unique urban plans, but also to their extraordinary settings — many rising on hilltops or among the complex gradients of the unpredictable Tuscan countryside, with its rolling farmlands tended with an elegance (the studied ranks of fields, olive groves and vineyards) rivaling that of the magnificent churches and palazzi in town. The Tuscan hills are invariably hospitable, without sharp or jutting peaks. In this domestic physiognomy, villas and farms seem to radiate from the towns themselves, eliminating any sense of a break between town and countryside. The old centers of many Tuscan towns are graced with towers from their commune days, echoes of the origins of Italian urban civilization; numerous churches vie with one another for the originality and beauty of their architecture. The emphasis is not only on Florence, but on places like Pistoia, Lucca, Pisa, Arezzo, and other small towns between the Tiber and Arno rivers, and between the Arno and the Orcia. Each town has its own personality, despite the centuries of influence and direct dominion of Florence through the Granduchy. Of major interest are the fortifications at Leghorn and Grosseto; here is a different kind of Tuscany, with something Tyrrhenian and peripheral compared to its historical heart. Towns throughout the region today show a great variety, stemming from the dynamism affecting certain areas and from the relative historical isolation of others. While there are no truly peripheral or isolated towns today, urban developments in modern times vary considerably from one end of the region to the other. Florence has remained the main city, and the surrounding plain is clogged with industrial expansion and new housing programs that have created a metropolitan organism engulfing Prato and Pistoia and beyond. To reach historic Florence, one has to get past various building cordons. Once beyond them, the old Florence abides — albeit assailed by tourists and choked with traffic — with its churches, its cupola, its Renaissance glories, its piazzas steeped in history and human travail, where at almost every corner the eye delights in its aesthetic and historical heritage. Our reading of Florence and the other towns populating Tuscany sheds light on the original developments of Italian history: the formation of contained city-states, their rivalry, and their eventual submission to the new state. The political unification of Italy drew a great deal of its cultural referents from Florence and Tuscany. Italy may not be Tuscany, but Tuscany is certainly the heart of Italy.

■ 72. A close-up of the facade of the Duomo, Lucca. Even a small detail like this is revealing of the style, the artistic and architectural ambitions typical to Tuscan towns, which developed a unique urban culture over several centuries, from the Middle Ages (to which the Duomo and other churches belong) through to the Renaissance. The urban splendors of Lucca are the outcome of its background of great economic prosperity (it enjoyed a thriving silk industry) and, from the fifteenth century, of its political independence. It remained a free republic for five centuries, with its own statutes. Lucca's local architectural style — explicit in the facade of the duomo, which was started in the thirteenth century — shows the local fondness for plastic decorative work, which drew on the expertise of artists from Pisa as well as that of the town's own stock.

■ 73. Piazza del Mercato, Lucca. This market square takes its oval shape from the foundations of the Roman amphitheater on which the medieval houses were built. Traces of the original stones can be found in the houses themselves, incorporated into the masonry. It is one of the best examples of how many Italian towns are the result of successive medieval and Renaissance grafts onto the original Roman settlements. Lucca's magnificent perimeter wall enclosing the medieval city in fact dates from the Renaissance, forming one of the greatest achievements of defense engineering in the country.

■ 74. Right: A view of the cathedral and baptistery, Pisa. The complex of monuments spread over the green carpet of Piazza dei Miracoli is quite unique. Set slightly outside the city's central nucleus, the graceful arrangement of the three features (the Duomo, the baptistery, and the famous leaning tower) and the matchless white Carrara marble used to build them are representative of a highly original vision of the city. This is better understood if one considers that, between the eleventh and fourteenth centuries, Pisa was a celebrated center for the arts, sanctioned by the economic prowess of the marine republic, which knew how to stand up against Genoa and Florence.

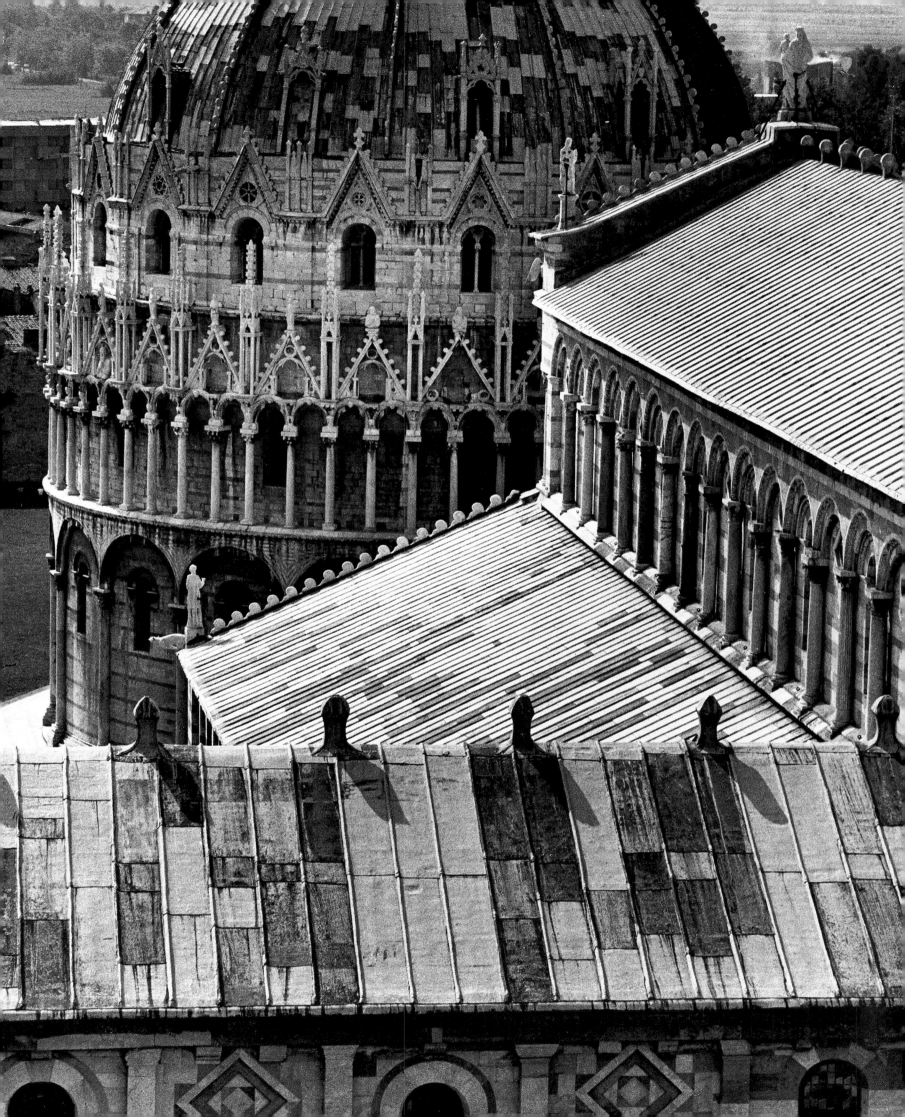

■ 75. Left: The baptistery of Pisa, whose slender, luminous features make it a monument of exceptional grace. The arches of the lower section are surmounted by a run of delicate smaller arches supporting richly ornamented pilaster cusps. The Romanesque plan of the baptistery is enhanced with ornaments in true Pisan Gothic style, a style that also spread further afield. Construction itself started in the twelfth century, during which period the Duomo was also completed.

■ 76. A detail of the pulpit made by Giovanni Pisano, kept in the church of Sant'Andrea in Pistoia. The composition depicts the Slaying of the Innocents. The church which houses this masterpiece, considered one of the pinnacles of achievement in Italian sculpture between the thirteenth and fourteenth centuries, is only one of the many signal works of art gracing the town. Owing to its striking townscapes and historical heritage, Pistoia ranks among the more famous Tuscan cities as a place to visit.

■ 77 & 78. Overleaf: Two views of Florence. Left: The Ponte Vecchio over the Arno river as it passes through the oldest quarter of town. This famous bridge was first built in the tenth century, then rebuilt in the fourteenth after a devastating flood. Even then, the bridge was host to characteristic goldsmiths' shopstalls lining either side; the jutting shops behind them, with their wooden support beams, were tacked on during the seventeenth century. Ponte Vecchio remains one of Florence's main attractions and has become a definitive part of the city's image. Right: The main fountain in Piazza della Signoria, with its statue of Neptune. This too is one of the monuments used to symbolize Florence, irrespective of the artistic worth of the work itself (nicknamed "Biancone," "white giant"), sculpted by Bartolomeo Ammannati. In the background stands the Palazzo della Signoria, also known as Palazzo Vecchio.

■ 79. A detail of Michelangelo's chapel, called the Sagrestia Nuova, in the basilica of San Lorenzo, Florence. This is an extraordinary jewel of the high Renaissance (1520–33) with its cogent pictorial exploitation of the various marbles employed and the poise and harmony of the whole, built on a square plan surmounted by a cupola. The chapel is host to the monumental tombs of Lorenzo II and Giuliano, of the Medici dynasty.

■ 80. Right: Florence's Duomo, alongside Santa Maria del Fiore. The construction of this monumental church was started in 1296 on the order of the Florentine republic, which spared no costs to endow the city with the "highest and most sumptuous invention such that no greater or more beautiful achievement of man's industry and power be possible." The first project was entrusted to Arnolfo di Cambio, but the Duomo was not consecrated until 1436, after various alterations to the original project and the completion of Brunelleschi's exquisite dome.

■ 81. Left: Piazza del Campo, Siena, seen from the Mangia tower at the city hall. The piazza is one of the most famous in the country, the theater for the yearly steeplechase. During this thrilling race (which dates back to the thirteenth century and has taken place each year, with the same rules, since 1656), the piazza becomes a kind of volcano, in which thousands and thousands of people cram together to get a share in the tension and excitement. Most of the spectators are locals come to cheer on the horse representing their own particular *contrada*. The sloping shell shape of the piazza makes it a unique, breathtaking setting. The shadow of the tower sweeps round the sectioned coping of the square like a giant sundial. Despite the variety of the frontage looking onto the piazza, the overall form is one of near perfection.

■ 82. Previous page, right: Flag-bearers outside the Duomo in Siena during the celebrations prior to the Palio steeplechase. The cathedral is just one of the marvels of Siena. Like the Palazzo Comunale (town hall), the cathedral is a reminder of the city's long period of independence as a free commune and then as a republic. Wars, sieges, and periodical subjection were unable to crush the spirit of the Sienese. It was not until midway through the sixteenth century that the city finally bowed to the expansionist thrust of its mighty neighbor, Florence; nor has Siena entirely lost its past tenacity in conserving its identity.

■ 83 & 84. A street in the Bruco *contrada* or neighborhood in Siena, lined by houses with clay-tiled roofs. This magnificent panorama taken from the top of the Mangia tower, eighty-eight meters high, affords a clear view of the development of the city, with its carefully planned series of concentric rings of streets intersected by radials configured around the two major poles of attraction, the Duomo and the city hall. The fine profile of the cathedral, with its horizontally striped dome, ornate facade cusps, and elegant belfry, looms up behind a sea of red roofs (right). The cathedral is an unusual, imposing building, quite detached from modern man's imagery. With its peculiar blend of Gothic and Romanesque genius, the Duomo was completed over the thirteenth and fourteenth centuries.

114

■ 85. A view of San Gimignano with its towers crowding the medieval enclave, gathered on the crest of a hill in the Val d'Elsa. Today those towers continue to symbolize the town's medieval heritage, largely lost to our age. Probably in the past they were an outspoken sign of wealth and pride, commanding respect from approaching travelers. A mere fifteen of the original seventy-two towers have survived; below them, the streets cut a dense web of grooves between ancient buildings, piazzas, and spaces that give a clear idea of the town in distant centuries. The perimeter wall, completed in the twelfth century, encloses the medieval burg, which has remained largely intact, though many of its buildings have been renovated or entirely rebuilt in the meantime.

■ 86. Piazza Pio II in the town of Pienza. This small town nestling in the hillside south of Siena is an astounding example of Renaissance town planning. The geography of the piazzas and streets is fascinating, and the way in which certain key buildings — especially Palazzo Piccolomini, a veritable gem of fifteenth-century architecture — fit into the urban fabric is most discerning. The cathedral shown, basically Renaissance in design but with strong Gothic elements, is the work of Bernardo Rossellino, who also directed works on the town plan commissioned by the humanist Enea Silvio Piccolomini (Pope Pius II).

■ 87 & 88. Two views of Arezzo, a Tuscan town that has held on to some considerable assets of its history, especially those from the era of the communes, during which it enjoyed great prosperity.
Left: The three upper loggias of the parish church of Santa Maria, considered one of the greatest achievements of Romanesque genius in Tuscany. Its construction was started in the twelfth century in the oldest nucleus of the town, itself founded on the plan of an Etruscan settlement. This picture shows the influence of the master-builders of Pisa and Lucca. Arezzo had its own master craftsmen, but these were largely sculptors.
Right: The apse of the cathedral, a Gothic construction begun at the end of the thirteenth century and finished two centuries later. The completion of this important building signaled the end of independence, as Arezzo passed to the dominion of the Florentines.

■ 89. The courtyard inside the Palazzo Pretorio, Cortona. This thirteenth-century complex was conceived as the residence of the Casali, a powerful local family who became the seigneurs of the town from the fourteenth to the fifteenth century. This walled medieval town, perched on the craggy heights of Sant'Egidio, conserves numerous remarkable monuments, churches, buildings, and streets, which all emanate a strong sense of history. In the more distant past the site was host to the Etruscans, who built the original walls and left many tombs. Archaeological finds from this period are on exhibit in the Museo dell'Accademia Etrusca, lodged in this building.

■ 90. A view of Piazza Garibaldi in Massa Marittima. This small town on the Maremma hillside overlooking the sea is one of the many surprises of Tuscany. The authentic feel of its streets and buildings, and especially its main square, is all the more intensified by the town's location off the beaten track; thus it has been spared the chaotic growth of many of its Tuscan counterparts. Massa Marittima grew on an Etruscan settlement, and after many years as a flourishing commune it passed to the Sienese and Florentines. The Duomo is its main treasure, built in the thirteenth century by master masons from Pisa. The square is crowned by other splendid buildings such as the Palazzo Vescovile, the Palazzo Pretorio, and the imposing Palazzo Comunale, the town hall.

THE CITIES OF UMBRIA AND THE MARCHES.
Medieval Isolation on the Ancient Hills

*T*he towns of Umbria and The Marches are all small or medium in size. Generally speaking, they did not experience major developments after the Middle Ages because they lie off the track beaten by major events in the history of the Italian peninsula; development was also impeded by centuries of papal dominion. Ensconced in the isolation of their mountain habitat, these villages and towns have preserved a rural economy handed down from the days of the communes. Only in this century have some of them finally been drawn out of their stasis and seclusion; but even today, visitors can experience the thrill of rediscovering Italy's archaic urban spirit, sculpted here in these remote streets and squares.

In many cases, the towns of Umbria and The Marches are like balconies or loggias looking out across the hills to the faraway peaks of Apennines — many in high locations, perched on mountainsides or high ledges. Assisi and Spello, for instance, command a view of the entire Umbra Valley. Perugia and Todi are also situated on peaks, where the town square offers a truly magical locus, with fine towers and the belfry of the main church. The towns and cities of The Marches are poised on the long chain of peaks that form the backbone of Italy. In both regions, sweeping views give a keen sense of the country's narrow peninsula form, with the sea on either side.

The predominant character of these cities is one of antiquity. Some have risen on top of early Etruscan towns (Perugia still has its original gates and tracts of the fortified wall), others on Roman cities (as with Assisi and Ascoli Piceno). These lofty sites bear the mark of centuries of settlement; the peaks themselves have become almost artificial after repeated efforts to shore them up and protect them from erosion (not always successfully, as can be seen at Orvieto, the town perched on a huge rock that is slowly splitting apart, threatening the stability of the ancient site). Each of these buttressed sites has its piazza, its churches and palaces recalling the fortunes of an earlier age or the enterprising mind of a nobleman, religious order, or community. While in most towns the spirit of the Renaissance and successive periods is manifest, the predominant style is medieval, as seen in the ancient centers of Spoleto, Todi, Gubbio, Assisi, Spello, Urbino, and Ascoli Piceno.

Assisi has a style of its own. For centuries this beautifully preserved town has been a sacred destination for pilgrimages to the shrine of Saint Francis. Despite the tourist facilities run by the friars, an atmosphere of deep spirituality survives here that is peculiar to Umbria, with its secluded townships. Even the countryside has different characteristics than those of neighboring Tuscany, with a more intense and arcane feeling for nature, perhaps, which the hillside towns seem to breathe even today.

The towns of The Marches tend to be affected by the closeness of the Adriatic Sea because of the gentle slope of the region toward the coast, which is dominated by thriving seaside towns such as Pesaro and Ancona. But the towns with the most magical and deepest history are to be found in the interior — towns such as Urbino, Macerata, and Ascoli Piceno, each one with a distinct history of its own but a common rapport with the central ridge of mountains and the nearby sea. And everywhere, the local conception of urban culture is expressed in the many admirable churches and palazzi.

■ 91. The Rocca Maggiore, or stronghold of Assisi, and, in the foreground, the dome of the cathedral. This Umbrian town is one of the fulcrums of Italy's glorious past civilization, a town of awesome monuments testifying to the Middle Ages and to the life and mystical vision of its patron, Saint Francis. Marvelously well preserved, Assisi is a busy tourist center and meeting point for pilgrims (two basically inseparable roles). Its monuments date back to both Roman and medieval times. The Middle Ages saw the reorganization of the town as a free commune, which subsequently passed through the hands of various nobles and thence to papal dominion. Thanks to this last period of isolation and decay, Assisi has remained virtually intact. The Rocca was built to the canons of Germanic feudalism (it was the residence of Frederick II), and largely rebuilt in the fourteenth century by order of the papal legate, Cardinal Albornoz. Assisi's main treasure is the basilica, one of the most important temples of all Christianity. Built in the thirteenth century, the basilica is the first great example of strictly Italian Gothic architecture, and contains the most prized series of frescoes from the thirteenth and fourteenth centuries.

■ 92 & 93. Two views of Perugia. Left: Via Baglioni, a passageway which follows the perimeter of the Rocca Paolina, a fortified complex built in the sixteenth century after the demolition of various medieval houses and towers. The Rocca is one of the most significant constructions of the current age, the last of a succession of buildings which have topographically transformed the hill on which the city rises, starting from the times of the Etruscans and Romans (witness the city walls and gates). Perugia has always played a vital role thanks to its position high above the upper Tiber Valley. It was a lively commune during the Middle Ages before passing to papal rule in the fourteenth century. Right: The historical fabric of the city is gathered on the hilltop, which gives the streets and squares an interesting geography, as seen from this street leading up into the heart of the old town, to Piazza IV Novembre and Corso Vannucci.

■ 94. Overleaf, left: A detail of the facade of San Nicola, the most prestigious historical building in Tolentino, a town cradled in the Chienti Valley in The Marches. The picture shows the upper section of the Renaissance Gothic portal, built in the fifteenth century by the Florentine Nanni di Bartolo. In addition to San Nicola, the town has preserved many important reminders of the communal age, a period during which it held out for a long time before becoming a seigneury and then submitting to papal dominion.

■ 95. Right: A corner of Urbino, showing the Palazzo Ducale looming over the medieval nucleus of the city. This monumental complex is the result of the insertion of the Renaissance concept of a palace into the fabric of the existing city as a homage to the rising ascendancy of the seigneuries throughout the country. The eminent historical building was commissioned by Frederick of Montefeltro, an enlightened prince who raised his family dynasty to great heights of fortune. The family owed its prestige to the hospitality they showed toward the great artists of the time. It was here in Urbino that the genius of Raphael and Bramante first began to develop. The glorious palace, standing proudly against the rolling hillside that slopes down toward the Adriatic, is an intricate structure which involved the work of various different architects and artists. Today it houses an important museum and a national collection of highly prized works of art.

■ 96. The skyline of Ascoli Piceno with its towers and belfries, some of which were reworked from earlier towers built by patrician families during the days when the city was a thriving free commune. But Ascoli's history actually goes much further back, to Roman times and its foundation by the Sabines, who called it *Asculum*. Even after its submission to the papacy, Ascoli continued to thrive off its brisk trade activities and rich agricultural land. The city's medieval legacy is well preserved, and likewise the constructions of later date, particularly those of the sixteenth century, when it fostered a highly reputable school of art that asserted itself even outside Ascoli. The urban fabric also abounds with Roman remains, making Ascoli the richest city for history and art in the entire region.

■ 97. Piazza della Libertà, in the center of Macerata. Visible on the right is the Palazzo della Prefettura and, in the background, the elegant Loggia dei Mercanti, built in fifteenth-century Tuscan style, alongside the town hall. Like the other historic buildings in Macerata, the town hall was also built with the pale-colored brick used throughout The Marches, which takes its color from the clay soil of the surrounding hillsides. The city, which was a free commune and first sided with the Ghibellines before becoming an episcopal seat, has a university dating from the thirteenth century.

■ 98. Left: The Palazzo dei Consoli in the Umbrian town of Gubbio. The building is one of Gubbio's most majestic monuments, and the main symbol of its past and its background as an independent city which clung to its freedom right through the age of the communes — from the eleventh century to the end of the fourteenth. During this period of prosperity the city was densely populated and was enhanced with several palaces, churches, and other buildings of great civic value. The Palazzo Ducale, however, was built in the fifteenth century, during the dominion of the Montefeltro dynasty that governed the city for some considerable time before it passed to papal rule in 1624. Gubbio's origins, which go back to the ancient settlement *Iguvium*, established by the Umbri tribe and subsequently taken over by the Romans, are testified to by the *Tavole Eugubine* in the Museo Comunale and by the Roman theater, one of the largest of its kind.

■ 99. A detail of the facade of San Pietro, near Spoleto. The motifs shown here are parts of the sculpted volutes and floral moldings adorning the posts that frame the main entrance. The church was built in the fifth century on an iron-age cemetery. Much of it was reworked in later stages, particularly in the thirteenth and fourteenth centuries. San Pietro is only part of the legacy of monuments in Spoleto, a city whose medieval heritage is virtually intact. But it also has other remnants of history, such as the various Roman monuments, aptly complemented by a charming urban context that harmonizes with the surrounding hills, which have only partly been ruined by new developments.

■ 100. The interior of the cathedral of San Ciriaco, Ancona. This Romanesque church with a Greek cross floorplan was built in the eleventh century on an earlier paleochristian church, itself built on a Roman temple dedicated to Venere Euplea, protectress of sailors. The church is perched on the summit of Mount Guasco, a crag that juts out toward, and offers a magnificent view of, the coast and the old port town, now an unbroken line of expansion stretching northward up the coast. Ancona has a very eventful past. During its heyday as a seafaring republic, the town was in constant conflict with Venice and with other towns in the interior, such as Jesi. In the sixteenth century it fell definitively under papal rule.

■ 101. A view of Jesi and a stretch of the walls girting the medieval nucleus. This town in The Marches has a lively history. The twelfth and fourteenth centuries were particularly eventful, when it was an enterprising and prosperous commune, though perpetually at war with its neighbors (especially with Ancona), and drained by internal struggles. In the sixteenth century it was taken over by the papacy and then for centuries it remained somewhat cloistered in its hilltop site, overlooking the sea. Today it is a hive of activity and industry, and has become one of the many central Italian towns in which the dense historical fabric cohabits with the ongoing building expansion fostered by ten years of intense economic growth.

THE CITIES OF LAZIO AND THE CENTRAL APENNINES.
The Hallmark of Rome

*F*ew cities can boast a historical heritage as rich and plenteous as Rome's. Basically, Rome is made up of four cities, one built over the other. The first was the ancient caput mundi, heart of the Roman civilization, whose unique ruins are still some of the most spectacular imaginable. The second Rome was the capital of Christianity, with its churches and clerical palaces: a Christianity that was more a question of display than a spiritual lifestyle, and whose monuments testify more to its dominion than to an inner spiritual path. The third Rome is the capital that grew alongside the seat of the Holy Catholic Church, a city of monuments to the political unification of Italy, with the ministries and head offices of the state administration. The fourth Rome is the city of the new residential quarters, the so-called borgata, which have provided the somewhat sparse, anonymous setting for that worldly-wise humor of Rome's poorer, lower-class generations who grew up in the shadows of the grand palaces of the papal lords. This more recent version of Rome is also a reservoir for former shepherds from the rural area south of the city and farm workers who gravitated from central and southern Italy, enhancing the "Roman-ness" of Rome and in turn succumbing to its extraordinary influence, as all who move to Rome are bound to do, one way or another. Here lies the sheer originality of the capital, the unshakable urban character whose roots run deep into the Rome of two thousand years hence. Perhaps this character stems from its central position on the peninsula and its two thousand years of experience as a capital, ventilated by the fresh breezes off the Tyrrhenian Sea and the Apennines.

The most striking feature of Rome, however, which has endured despite the more recent transformations that have made Rome an industrial and service-sector mecca in addition to its bureaucratic functions, is the city's role as the papal capital, modeled by the culture of its aristocracy, whose power in past centuries irradiated through the papal state and outward, through the region of Lazio, where the presence of Rome is inescapable. Scattered through Lazio are innumerable small towns where the cultural customs of urban life have been grafted onto Etruscan and Roman traditions, where the mansions of the papal princes rise on what were formerly Etruscan lucomonie or Roman villas: Tarquinia, Viterbo, Orvieto, Sulmona, L'Aquila, just as other towns grew around Roman and pre-Roman legacies, witnesses to the ancient history of this stretch of land spanning from the Tyrrhenian Sea to the Apennine hills. The region's more typical towns tend to be on the tufaceous slopes of northern Lazio, in the volcanic area where the Etruscan forerunners laid the foundations for a new culture that blended Apennine, highland mores with those of Tyrrhenian, maritime inclination, and left an important legacy to the Romans. Likewise, on the mountain slopes overlooking the Lazio lowlands, towns of smaller dimensions like Tivoli, Anagni, and Alatri are also scored with the deep imprints of history.

Another form of urban culture, a projection of the Roman idea of the borgata, can be found in the resorts along the Tyrrhenian coastline. Here, development came with the draining of the malaria-infested swamplands. The reclaiming of this land, whose scenario of shifting livestock so caught the imagination of the foreign traveler, was carried out under Fascism. This period also saw the foundation of new towns which bear the indelible mark of the ruling ideas, such as Sabaudia and Latina. On the city outskirts and along the coast, where the towns and villages still betray the layout of the original Roman settlement, more recent developments have created urban landscapes that look like a projection of the capital itself. Though they throb with the liveliness of the Mediterranean, these towns are chaotic and ill-planned, typical characteristics of this part of the country.

■ 102. Relics of the Etruscan cemetery of Tarquinia, scattered across the surrounding plains. The cemetery offers important insights on the civilization of the Etruscans, on their way of life and their feelings on existence and death. The tombs are very numerous and yielded a wealth of burial goods when excavation started at the end of the eighteenth century (though their existence was known as early as the fifteenth century). They mainly date back to the era in which Tarquinia, a powerful, thriving Etruscan town since the ninth century B.C., expanded through Rome and the Campania region from the seventh to fifth centuries B.C. Most of the material recovered from the tombs is now found in the national museum at Tarquinia in the Palazzo Vitelleschi, a monumental building in Renaissance Gothic style.

■ 103. A decorative motif on the facade of the town hall of Narni. Though in Lazio, the town has close links with nearby Umbria through the ancient causeway, the Via Flaminia, which linked Rome to the upper Adriatic. Narni thrived particularly in the twelfth century, when it took a brave stand against the papacy in a bid to secure its own independence. Important medieval buildings include the Palazzo del Podestà, the magnificent Duomo, and the thirteenth-century Romanesque church of Santa Maria Impensale. The hilltop nucleus of the old town commands a splendid view of the Nera river valley.

■ 104. Right: A detail of the Palazzo Papale, the most important early building in Viterbo. Its striking loggia of complex arches form one section of the building constructed in the thirteenth century. Viterbo boasts an abundance of medieval and later monuments, and its history is closely tied to the papacy. On various occasions it was the papal capital, and consequently was party to many key historical events. Viterbo's roots go back much further, however, to the Etruscan settlement and later Roman town. The townscape is memorable for the dark hues of the building material, a local volcanic tufa.

■ 105. Overleaf: The right flank of the Duomo of Orvieto, judged to be one of Italy's most beautiful churches. Construction began at the end of the thirteenth century and took several centuries to complete. Many artists and architects from all over the country contributed to the work. The original plan was Romanesque; its present splendid Gothic form, with its fine marble profile towering over the medieval burg poised on the summit of a huge crag of tufa overlooking the Paglia river, is more recent. Other churches and palaces of considerable architectural merit can be found through the town. There are also important traces of the Etruscans everywhere on the hilltop, confirming the town's eventful historical background.

■ 106 & 107. Two views of Rome. Right: Inside the Colosseum, the most awe-inspiring relic of ancient Rome and the main symbol of the city's imperial heritage. For centuries, travelers to Italy have gazed in wonder at the ancient stones. Built in the first century A.D., the amphitheater has a maximum span of 188 meters and a height of 44 meters. The original tiered seating could accommodate no less than fifty thousand spectators. The Colosseum was built to match the proportions of the capital, which in those days is estimated to have harbored a million souls. Right: The Neptune fountain in Piazza Navona. Fountains are an important feature of the Roman townscape. Here they add a touch of grandeur to Piazza Navona, one of Rome's most scenic public squares, built over the plan of a Roman circus and surrounded by superb churches and buildings, with three fountains featuring mythological scenes.

■ 108 & 109. Two more views of Rome. Right: In the foreground, Santa Maria di Montesanto e dei Miracoli, with the dome of San Pietro (Saint Peter's) behind it. The dome is the first thing one sees of the head church of Christianity, the "church of churches." Its image is engraved in the memory of half of humanity. Designed by Michelangelo in the early sixteenth century, the majestic dome looms above the capital, giving the cityscape a style of mixed Renaissance and baroque genius against a backdrop of vestiges of ancient Rome. The charm of the city (when one can get away from the traffic congestion) lies in this strange marriage of eras, in its continuity as a capital despite the changes in architectural and urban styles. A fine example is the Trinità dei Monti with its steps up the Pincio hill, majestic but welcoming at the same time. The flights of steps were designed by Francesco De Sanctis, and completed in the first half of the eighteenth century, the period responsible for many other major baroque works throughout the city. Rome is also the capital of baroque art, which found an ideal setting among the hills and ancient ruins.

■ 110. The medieval burg of Sant'Erasmo, Gaeta, with its castle, cathedral belfry, and its old houses huddled round the port of Santa Maria. The cathedral complex commands the tip of a promontory dominated by Mount Orlando, beyond which lies modern Gaeta and the port of Sant'Antonio. Due to the defiant slopes of the promontory, Gaeta has always played strategic and military roles. Its origins go back to the Roman settlement of Caita, mentioned by Virgil in the *Aeneid*. In the Middle Ages the town suffered countless sieges, passing from one dominion to another — the Moors, Normans, Aragons, Popes, French, and Bourbons each at one time had control of the town. In 1860–61 the Bourbons made it their last bastion against the Italian forces. While modern Gaeta is a bustling town, the ancient burg on the promontory, the scene of a vibrant military past, is run-down and almost deserted.

■ 111. The splendid second-century aqueduct in Piazza Garibaldi, Sulmona. This hillside town was important during Roman times because of its position along the main corridor through the Apennines. Sulmona reached its peak in medieval times, particularly during the thirteenth century, when it won the favor of Frederick II of Swabia. It managed to keep its independence through to the next century, when it became a feud of the large princely families under the papacy. The town bears many fine reminders of the past, including some from Roman times. Its heritage includes the magnificent Romanesque basilica, derived from an earlier building of ninth-century foundation, and splendid palazzi built in the course of the ensuing centuries. The broad valley situation of the town is now host to numerous factories. The town itself commands a central position, the variety of its monuments and mature civil atmosphere testifying to the level of culture that even remoter towns, like this mountainside town, managed to reach by the Middle Ages, drawing invariably upon their remote Roman ancestry.

■ 112. The vestiges of Emperor Hadrian's palace at Villa Adriana, Tivoli, on the outskirts of Rome. The remains of the main plan and the surviving buildings at this archaeological site give a clear sense of the magnificence of the emperor's world when Rome was at the apex of its glory. The villa was commissioned by Hadrian (who drafted most of the plan himself) and built over the period A.D. 118–34. Excavation work and restoration of the ruins began as far back as the end of the fifteenth century, by papal order. Besides the beauty of the monuments, the setting itself is sublime and draws a constant stream of visitors.

■ 113. The so-called "fountain of the ninety-nine conduits" at L'Aquila. This curious fountain is one of the many interesting historical features of the Apennine town, most of which date from the thirteenth century. During that time, the town swelled to accommodate people from the castles and hamlets scattered through the Aterno valley who were fleeing the exploitation of the feudal lords. The original burg was soon girdled by a host of small neighborhoods, each representing one of the ninety-nine feudal castles (the same number of conduits in the fountain, and the number of strokes made by the town bells). Churches, palazzi, and the castle (one of the principal monuments) are reminders of the erstwhile role of the town across the territory, though it never grew to any appreciable size due to its somewhat entrenched site in the mountainous interior of the peninsula. In contrast, the town's development this century as a provincial capital and focus of various kinds of industrial activity has been rapid.

THE CITIES OF THE SOUTH. Mediterranean Humanity and Dissipation

*M*ore than anywhere else in the country, the cities and towns of the south have direct links with their historical forerunners. Pompeii, Herculaneum, Paestum, and other archaeological sites have granted us a wonderfully realistic view of life in ancient Roman and Graeco-Roman towns. What links today's city with those of the past? At Pompeii in particular one can almost hear the voices, the bustling and bartering of the past, against the azure backdrop of the Tyrrhenian Sea — surely no different from the animated scenarios to be found all along the Bay of Naples today. The layout and functions of today's cities may have changed, but the genuine Mediterranean feel of their social life, the theatrical, pagan hubbub, the doleful sensuality, are probably much the same.

As remarked by travelers during the last century, Naples had an unforgettable allure and offered the most authentic concentration of the bubbling southern spirit. Today's traveler inevitably finds Naples the epitome of the impotent urban agglomeration, plagued by blight and utterly unlivable. Contemporary Naples is symbolic of the south's inability to keep up with the rest of Italy, to adapt to the progressive spirit of our times. And yet eighteenth-century Naples was not simply a series of picturesque, golden seascapes, a mecca for foreign visitors. It was a full-fledged city with a vibrant urban culture of its own making. With its baroque palazzi, fine monuments, and fervid artistic life, the city was the capital of the Kingdom of Naples: although in the hands of a decadent and squandering aristocratic class, it was not lacking in enterprise and active participation in the political and cultural vagaries of Europe. The city had instigated the drive to abolish the feudal system and the creation of a new social order, but the outcome was a bitter disappointment to its proponents. The feuds quickly turned into dominions in the hands of barons and titled landlords, engendering ranks of destitute farmworkers without producing an enterprising middle class that could pit itself against the baronial power and construct a new, more dynamic civic reality.

Other cities in the south convey this sense of failure to regenerate the urban culture. From Campania and Apulia to Basilicata, the smaller and medium-sized towns vaunt their enduring legacy of baronial mansions, castles, and wonderful churches, but outside the enclave of historic buildings the town is uniform and drab, despite the general rise in the bourgeois role of administration ushered in by the political unification of the country and the burgeoning middle class of property holders. Urban patterns show bands of growth encircling the original nucleus and merging with amorphous areas of more modern expansion, as in Naples and Salerno. Apulia, Bari, Brindisi, Taranto, and Lecce have become full-blown cities, and yet they have somehow kept the overall layout typical of medium-sized towns. The urban model is much the same, too: an anonymous band of new development crowning a historical core of fairly precise regional character — narrow streets and Romanesque churches, or rows of seafront cottages. What marks the highly original urban pattern of the towns of Apulia is the cogent dialogue with the surrounding countryside.

Among the marvelous patchwork of southern towns, there are some that constitute a model apart. One of these is Caserta, with its regal palace of the Bourbon dynasty, designed as a mini-Versailles; Benevento, with its magnificent relics of ancient Rome; Amalfi, which harks back to the glorious days of the marine republics which stood their ground with the Arab trading hegemony; and finally the most curious of all southern towns, Matera, with its historic center built around a set of cell-dwellings carved into the cliff, originally the caves of early Christian hermits.

■ 114. The cloister of Santa Chiara, Naples. All the surfaces, pillars and benches included, are decorated with majolica tiles depicting mythological scenes and floral motifs. The cloister, called the Chiostro delle Clarisse — part of a remarkable church complex built in the early fourteenth century and drastically reworked during the eighteenth century — was much frequented by the Neapolitan nobility.

It is attached to the neighboring convent, built at the same time as the main church. The majolica dates from the eighteenth century, when Neapolitan art was flourishing, and is emblematic of the prevailing Hispanic fondness for a characteristically Mediterranean play of color and ornamentation. Naples itself is wild and unruly, noisy and extrovert, but contains many quiet, unexpected corners of gentleness such as this

cloister. Its appeal lies in these surprises and in the Mediterranean glow of the light and the bursting sense of life, defiant of the innumerable problems of existence.

■ 115. The "Guglia dell'Immacolata," a monumental spire in true Neapolitan baroque style erected in Piazza del Gesù during the eighteenth century in place of an equestrian statue of the Bourbon king, Philip V, which was torn down by the population. The spire is typical of the monumental style found throughout the city, which, despite works from different periods and some signal historical artifacts, is predominantly baroque, as testified by the many churches dutifully commissioned by the nobility over the seventeenth and eighteenth centuries. The beautifying of Naples went hand-in-hand with the rise in its population and the related problems of urbanization, which were never really tackled by the various Bourbon sovereigns.

■ 116. On the preceding page: The rows of fountains in the park of the Reggia or royal palace of Caserta. The entire design testifies to the period in which sovereigns followed France and the French royalty in everything they did, from their methods of government to the royal architecture. The Reggia was built to designs by Vanvitelli between 1752 and 1774, and was a considerable drain on the coffers of the Bourbon dynasty.

■ 117. The ruins of Pompei's orthogonal street network. Pompeii gives the visitor an immediate sense of what the original city was like, with its strong sense of structure and functional arrangement of buildings — the hotels (*hospitia*), restaurants (*cauponae*), stables (*stabula*), and homes of wealthy families with their characteristic courtyards. We owe its conservation to the layer of ash and lava that engulfed the city when Vesuvius erupted on August 24, A.D. 79. The streets and houses, and the people and objects in them were brought to light just as they were on that fateful summer's day. The entire excavation area is an abiding testament. Pliny the Younger recorded the eye-witness account of his uncle, Pliny the Elder, of the eruption: "The ninth day before the calendar month of September, at roughly the seventh hour, my mother remarked to [Pliny the Elder] that a cloud of extraordinary dimensions and form had appeared on the horizon. ... Its appearance is best described as being that of a pine tree." This was a presage of the explosion that destroyed Pompeii, a thriving town taken over by the Romans in the first century B.C. The first excavations were made in 1748, but scientific studies did not really start until 1860 and are still

being carried out. Only part of the town has been brought to light.

■ 118. The Duomo of Amalfi, a lofty, luminous construction, reworked on various occasions. The layout of the original ninth-century church was quite different from today's distinctly mixed Arab-Norman plan. The belfry on the left was erected during the thirteenth century. The Duomo is one of the only remaining monuments to the fascinating past of Amalfi, which was a small but thriving marine republic between the ninth and twelfth centuries, when it managed to secure lively trade links with the Arab world. A set of marine regulations known as the Tavole Amalfitane were observed throughout the Mediterranean until the sixteenth century. The republic followed democratic principles, and was headed by *comites* or prefects who were elected each year, though power subsequently took on a dynastic form, with prefects holding their position indefinitely. Tightly hemmed in as it was on the coastline, Amalfi nonetheless managed to command a leading role in sea affairs and trade throughout the Tyrrhenian Sea.

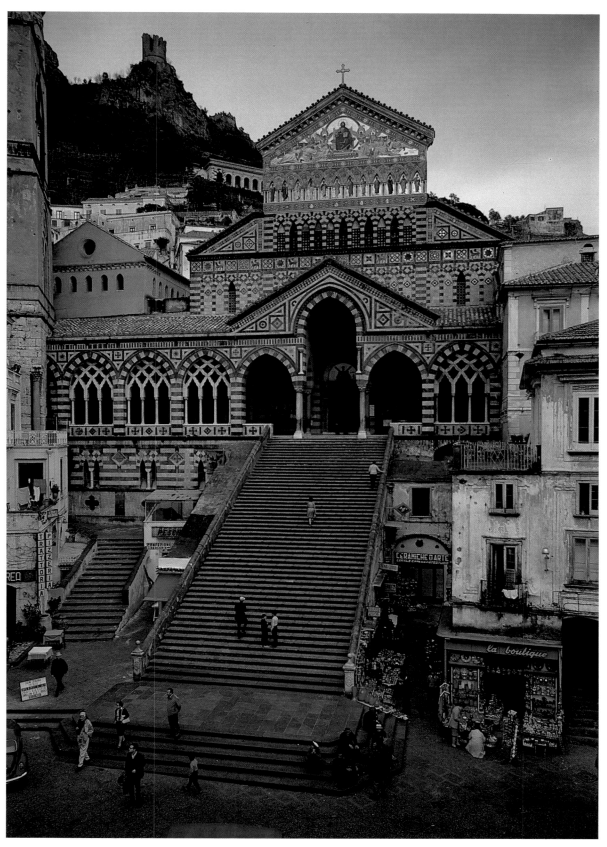

■ 119. The construction of the Roman theater in Benevento, dubbed the "grottoni" or grottoes. This is only one of the many relics of the town's memorable past, originally in the control of the Samnites until the Romans took it over in the early third century B.C. Its role increased in importance, as can be seen from the magnificent arch in memory of Trajan, one of the best preserved arches in Italy, erected in 114 B.C. to commemorate the opening of the Via Traiana which finished in Brindisi, like its more famous consular causeway, Via Appia (the Appian Way). Benevento maintained its importance in medieval times, too, when it became the capital of the Longobard duchy that dominated most of southern Italy from the sixth to the ninth century.

■ 120. One of the Sassi or old dwellings gouged into the rockface in Matera. Not all the cells have arches and walls in masonry; most show the exposed tufa stone from which they were excavated. Nearly all have architectural facades, with pediments, loggias, and balconies. The Sassi, no longer used as dwellings, line the cliff-face at the junction of two valleys (Sasso Caveoso and Sasso Barisano). Of signal architectural value, they were not abandoned until midway through the 1900s. Some were made into hypogeum-type churches in the style of Byzantine monks' cells, but most were used as living quarters, workshops, or storage units. As they emptied, the town over the valley began to flesh out, rather anonymously.

■ 121. Left: The castle of Taranto. This imposing fortress, built in the fifteenth century by order of Ferdinand of Aragon, commands the extreme eastern corner of the island on which the old city stands, and overlooks the channel linking Taranto's inland bay, the Mar Piccolo, with the Mar Grande and open sea. Owing to its protected site in the Bay of Taranto, the town was important even in classical times, and became one of the most flourishing centers of Magna Graecia. In more modern times it was a much-coveted military outpost, and to this day is the largest Italian naval base in the country, together with La Spezia.

■ 122. The facade of Santa Croce, Lecce. The church is considered the town's finest example of baroque architecture, the predominant style used throughout the historic center. The church's construction lasted from the sixteenth to the seventeenth century, a period that witnessed the completion of numerous other baroque buildings, all built with the beautiful local limestone, a clear, malleable material that lent itself well to the skills of the stonemasons of the period.

■ 123. The Colonne steps in Brindisi. At the top of the steps, a marble column twenty meters high, originally flanked by a second, marks the end of the Appian Way. In Roman times the port of *Brindisium* provided a valuable landing stage from whence ships embarked for the shores of Illyria, Greece, and the Orient. Various ancient historians and writers mention the town and the many key events that took place there, including the siege mounted by Julius Caesar in 49 B.C. During the Middle Ages it was a point of departure for the Holy Land and saw the embarkment of the Sixth Crusade. Brindisi's links with the eastern Mediterranean continue to be of vital interest to the town, which is also the headquarters of industries involved in the transformation of imported raw materials (chemical and oil products).

■ 124. A view of Gallipoli, one of the most enchanting "white" towns of Apulia. The photograph shows the original nucleus of the town, with its typical network of tight, winding streets. The old town grew on an island, now connected with the mainland and the more modern section of town by means of an artificial isthmus. In the foreground is the fort with its characteristic ravelin or outwork extending into what was the old port (Seno del Canneto). The sixteenth-century fort was built on the site of earlier fortifications. Gallipoli's history goes back a long way. A former colony of Taranto (*Callipolis*), it was stormed by the Romans in 266 B.C. In the Middle Ages it was annexed to the Byzantine Empire before its conquest by the Normans in the eleventh century. Today it thrives on its brisk agricultural assets inland and provides a major trading center for the busy Salento region.

■ 125. A building in the town of Martina Franca, with characteristic ironwork balustrades in true baroque style. The atmosphere of this typical "white" Apulian town stems largely from buildings like this, formerly the town houses of landed gentry. In the summer the glare of the white housefronts is dramatically contrasted by the vibrant greens of the Murge hillside. The town's character rests in this established urban spirit, although the economy, as with the rest of Apulia's towns, has always depended on farming. The core of Martina Franca is girded by the fourteenth-century perimeter wall, built by Philip of Anjou to protect the inhabitants drawn to the town by the special exemptions accorded by their sovereign.

■ 126. Right: The splendid series of arches gracing the side of the basilica of San Nicola, Bari. Together with the nearby cathedral, San Nicola is the masterpiece of the historic town center of Apulia's regional capital. The church was built in the eleventh century — according to a conception that has made it the head of Apulia's basilicas, also for the way it binds the people to political power — to house the body of its patron saint, brought here by local sailors from distant Lycia. To this day the saint is venerated and his translation to Bari is celebrated each year with a lively pageant.

■ 127 & 128. Overleaf: The old Duomo of Molfetta (left), with its characteristic trio of domes and lateral towers. Construction began in the eleventh century and continued into the thirteenth. The Duomo is truly one of the original examples of Apulian Romanesque, intimately woven with the old town's fabric around the harbor. Right: The apse of Trani cathedral, another masterpiece of Romanesque inspiration (twelfth-thirteenth century). With its tapering spire, the cathedral is an unusual combination of volume and glowing stone, and continues to be one of the principal artistic landmarks of Apulian urban culture.

162

■ 129. A view across Ostuni in the Murge hillside in Apulia, looking out to sea. Over the white houses of the original medieval settlement with their flat roofs (today bristling with television aerials) looms the fine cathedral. Such towns are a lasting example of the urban style common to the region — the narrow streets and clustered buildings are reminiscent of their Moorish counterparts on the Mediterranean coastline. Although its roots go back to classical times, apart from the Norman fortifications the town's history was thankfully uneventful.

■ 130. Right: The inner staircase of the sanctuary of San Michele in Monte Sant'Angelo. This small town is perched high on a hilltop with a view far across the Gargano countryside to the gulf of Manfredonia. The town's striking layout presents a maze of little houses with sloping roofs, connected by steep streets and stairways, with frequent terraces allowing a breathtaking view. The sanctuary itself is one of the oldest in Christendom, and draws pilgrims all year round, not only from Apulia. San Michele Arcangelo was founded late in the sixth century on a former monastery of the order of Saint Basil, and soon became the "national sanctuary" of the Longobards. The Moorish armies laid waste to the complex, but it later became a stepping stone for the Holy Latin Church's drive toward the east.

THE CITIES OF SICILY. A Sense of Insularity

*U*rban culture in Sicily began with Magna Graecia. Civilization on the island reached heights of unparalleled refinement, as testified in surviving classical texts and by the awe-inspiring ruins of the ancient cities unearthed by archaeologists. The Hellenic world found Sicily a fertile soil for its genius, and at one stage the island was one of the most intense cultural focuses of the entire Mediterranean. Sicily's coastal settlements were a tribute to the Hellenic world, and many of today's towns and cities crystallized around their foundations. In that remote past, Sicily's insularity never caused isolation or retrenchment, but rather responsiveness to the outside world and a talent for reworking exogenous cultural influences. In fact, the island's vantage point at the center of the Mediterranean helped forge an outgoing temperament in the inhabitants. Sicily's importance began to ebb as the cultural epicenter shifted northward from the Mediterranean basin to Europe. Subsequently the island experienced a succession of foreign sovereigns, including the Bourbon dynasty, which brought barons, an aristocratic culture, and resplendent baroque churches. The feudal stranglehold was inexorable and the hallmark of the ancien régime seemed indelible. Even when the island participated in the Unification, it remained locked in its immutable, anachronistic order. "In Sicily," explains the main character in Tomasi di Lampedusa's famous novel The Leopard, "all change is merely apparent. It simply reinstates the established order." This may have effectively safeguarded the island's specific character and qualities, but it has also made it insular and parochial. Today Sicily is a kind of satellite to the rest of Italy, resistant to any sense of nationalism or cohesion to the state.

Recent transformations in Sicilian life have not brought about a new order, as is plain from the island's towns and cities. Palermo, with its background of antiquity and nobility, its vivacious atmosphere, at once outgoing and cloistered, is a city that ceased to be a capital and degenerated into a Mediterranean sprawl. The plight of Catania, with its unique local architecture of dark volcanic rock silhouetted against the backdrop of Mount Etna, is much the same. The inland towns are the product of centuries of sedimented urban culture on the sites of ancient Greek and Roman settlements. Nearly all command a high position, looking out to sea or across to another lofty aggregation of houses, which are generally small, set in tight rows, and inhabited by farm laborers. Until recently these Sicilian towns (authentic "peasant towns") accommodated farmhands who worked daily on the huge estates, which they reached on the back of a donkey. That kind of town is no more. Agriculture has been streamlined and Sicily's Mediterranean products are increasingly competitive. Here and there, industrial plants have sprung up, and initiatives of all kinds have finally brought money to the old farming villages.

Throughout Sicily the townscape is frequently punctuated with imposing palazzi and baroque churches of extraordinary charm, a reminder of the days when the island, although somewhat distant from the heart of Europe, nonetheless enjoyed periods of enlightened government and culture on the part of its noble class. The people who control most of the island today, however, are of a very different stock. They dictate the growth or decay of the cities, calling the shots in both financial and real-estate sectors. But the towns and cities are well populated, alive with social bonds unseen elsewhere. The sense of social bonding goes beyond the powers of the state or even those of the Mafia, and each town is like a beehive, a biological organism that spontaneously re-adapts itself with no apparent design imposed from outside.

■ 131. A view of Messina, seen from the straits separating it from the Italian mainland, showing its rows of houses along the shoreline and the cliffs at the foot of the Peloritani hills. Messina, the main landing stage for the island, was originally a Greek settlement and remained a major seaport through the centuries thanks to its key position overlooking the mythical stretch of water separating the island from the continent. But the city itself is conspicuously of more recent design. The old city was completely razed in 1908 by a terrible earthquake. Only 4 percent of the building stock escaped with what was termed "light" damage; consequently, all the city's heritage was destroyed. Reconstruction began almost immediately, and all new buildings had to comply with strict earthquake-proofing standards. Today Messina is a brisk, leading seaport with a wide range of commercial activities. But it lacks that typically Sicilian gloss, the hallmark of eighteenth-century culture found in all the eastern towns of the island, which have been spared serious earthquakes since the seventeenth century.

■ 132. A street in Erice, a medieval town poised on the crest of a peak overlooking the western coast of Sicily. Erice was famous in Roman and Greek times for its temple dedicated to Aphrodite (Venus). Its tight weave of cobblestone streets and sudden clearings, and its courtyards and limestone buildings give the town a most unusual atmosphere. It is a traditional port-of-call for tourists and visitors, which has inevitably eroded the peaceful, cloistered character it once enjoyed.

■ 133. The cathedral square in the heart of Catania, with its characteristic fountain and elephant statue (known locally as Liotru), an eighteenth-century work whose lower statues represent the rivers Simeto and Amenano. The Duomo itself is one of Catania's main attractions, also dating from the eighteenth century but built on the ruins of earlier buildings (the first of which originated in the eleventh century) destroyed by successive earthquakes. The entire city, despite its Greek origins and impressive history, is distinctly baroque in flavor. It was largely rebuilt after the disastrous earthquake of 1693 that struck the entire southeastern coast of Sicily. Towering behind the city is Mount Etna, eternally threatening but at the same time a comforting sentinel.

■ 134. Left: Palazzo Beneventano dal Bosco, one of Syracuse's more sumptuous baroque marvels. This city also reflects the predominant eighteenth-century flavor typical of southeastern Sicily. But it has something extra, distinct echoes of its role in Ancient Greece as one of the most important cultural centers of the Mediterranean, and later as a vital Roman city. This distant past lives on in its many ancient ruins, which have survived the ongoing development of the modern city.

■ 135. The clustered housing of the older section of Ragusa, with its wealth of medieval and baroque buildings, built on the site of an ancient Greek settlement. Ragusa also suffered heavy damage during the 1693 earthquake, after which a "new" town was built on another shelf of the spur on which the original, centuries-old town of Ragusa Ibla tenaciously perches.

■ 136. The church of San Giorgio (also known as Chiesa Madre), a proud building dominating the old town center of Modica clustered below the peaks of the Iblei hills. This church, built at the beginning of the eighteenth century to the design of Rosario Gagliardi, is a condensation of a style that was popular in southeastern Sicily at the time. The result is a spectacular, luminous creation, resonant with Mediterranean and Spanish inspiration. It is set in the center of a town which, with its panoply of baroque buildings and complex perspectives, is one of the gems of Sicily.

■ 137. Right: The church of San Francesco and the monastery of Santissimo Salvatore in Noto, Sicily. This complex is situated in one of the island's finest baroque towns. The sheer variety of form is complemented by the warm, golden hues of the stone used in all its buildings. Regrettably, it is the kind of stone that crumbles, posing serious problems of conservation. Noto is actually something of a dream town; it was built to replace the previous settlement, which was razed by the 1693 earthquake. The designs were made by a scholar of the day (assisted by renowned architects working in the Ragusa area), mindful of the legacy of the great masters of Sicilian baroque inspiration.

■ 138 & 139. Norman relics at Palermo. Left: A view of the cathedral with the arcade running along its right flank. The cathedral's history is a useful inventory of certain important chapters in the life of the city. It was erected in the twelfth century on the site of a basilica that was transformed into a mosque during the Arab dominion, and restored to Christianity by the Normans. Despite the many alterations and additions made to the building, its current form is cohesive; its individual style involves a medley of Arab, Norman, and Catalan Gothic motifs. The cathedral commands the center of the old town, whose characteristic Arab layout is cut through with straight streets flanked by churches and palazzi of great dignity, though the townscape is generally in disrepair.

Right: The interior of the Martorana (Santa Maria dell'Ammiraglio), one of Palermo's most important monuments to Norman craftsmanship. The influence of Arab architecture is evident in the clean geometries and crystalline purity of form. It was built in the twelfth century with the assistance of Arab stonemasons, whose presence in Sicily during Norman supremacy has left the country with unmistakable traces of their culture.

■ 140. The ruins of the Greek theater in Taormina. Part of the town is just visible in the background and, higher up, the castle on the brow of Mount Tauro. The charisma of Taormina, which has dazzled untold numbers of foreign travelers, lies in its magical combination of ancient stone, the glistening sea it looks onto, the view of Mount Etna (snow-capped for several months of the year), the fragrance of the vegetation, and the uncanny, tropical light. Originally founded by Siculian tribesmen, Taormina was a town of Magna Graecia before becoming a Roman colony. During the Middle Ages it saw various forms of government, until decline set in around the fifteenth century.

■ 141. The apse of the Duomo of Monreale. The complex includes the cloister of the adjoining Benedictine convent, and is the finest example of Norman architecture in Sicily. Commissioned by William II of Sicily, the building has been spared major alterations and is therefore a rarity. Originally, its surroundings must have been impressive, given the view over the Conca d'Oro, the bay of Palermo.

■ 142. A panoramic view of Trapani on the west coast of Sicily. Despite the town's roots in the distant past, its present appearance is largely modern, though there are some relics of its medieval days and a few baroque churches and palazzi. The historical area is gathered on a curved promontory, while the more modern part has spread through the small catchment area below the hillside town of Erice. Trapani has a busy seaport serving the Egadi islands just off the coast, and administers the surrounding farmland, which supports a fair number of wine vineyards. There is also a nearby salt-works that has been active for centuries.

■ 143. Right: The famous flight of steps in Caltagirone, connecting the church of Santa Maria del Monte with the main town square. Visually stunning, the steps — devised by the architect Giuseppe Giacalone — are a major attraction in this populous inland town, whose name derives from the Arabic, *Qualat-el-Geluna*, and is famous for its centuries-old production of fine majolica.

Index to Illustrations